HIKING THE HIGH WALLOWAS AND HELLS CANYON

Revised Edition

edited by Frank Conley

PIKA PRESS
Enterprise, Oregon

Cover photograph of Eagle Cap by David Jensen
Maps adapted from US Forest Service maps.

PIKA PRESS
P.O. Box 457
203 1/2 E. Main
Enterprise, OR 97828

PREFACE TO THE REVISED EDITION

Hiking the High Wallowas was first published in 1988. The idea for the book started with conversation in the back room/coffee shop at the Bookloft in Enterprise. I owned the bookstore and a fledgling Pika Press. Mike Bohannon was the chairman of a local group called the "Wallowa Valley Resource Council." Frank Conley, who grew up in nearby Cove and had built trail, hiked, and fished over much of the territory, agreed to edit.

We came up with a format and sent off a small army of volunteers — Resource Council members and off-duty Forest Service workers — to hike, make notes, and take pictures. At the end of the hiking season Frank took all of the field notes and pictures and typed them into a coherent book. We printed 3000 copies and they sold out. We've been talking about revising and reprinting for over three years.

After a few unsuccessful attempts at that revised edition by various people, Frank Conley decided to "just do it." Frank has used the spring to revisit trailheads and check where forest fires may have impacted hiking areas. He's made necessary corrections and cleaned up the text. But substantially, we're walking the same ground we did in 1988. We'll wait until the third edition to add miles and trails.

The Wallowa Resource Council no longer exists, and some of the original hikers, who should still get credit for their part in this book, are no longer in the area. Doug and Robin Sims are in Alaska; Mike Bohannon is back in school in Corvallis; Robin Rose is in Baker City; and Doris Tai is on the Gifford Pinchot Forest. Laurel Reuben, Ken Witty, Ric Bailey, Stanlynn Daugherty, Bill George, Jan Hohmann, Janie Tippett, and Bob Jackson are all still living and hiking locally.

This revised edition is for them, and for those of you who are just discovering the Wallowas. Good hiking!

Rich Wandschneider

Pika Press
April 1995

CONTENTS

HIKE INDEX

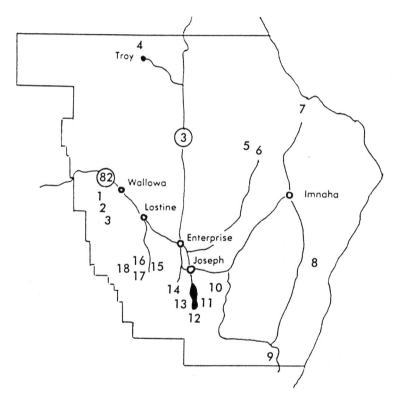

Wallowa County

Lower Imnaha River near confluence with the Snake.
(Janie Tippett photo)

INTRODUCTION

Wallowa County, the most northeastern county in Oregon, harbors some of the most spectacular, yet least publicized, backcountry in North America. From the central Wallowa Valley, the landscape is dominated by the granitic and incredibly steep and rugged rimrock and grasslands of the Grande Ronde River Canyon to the northwest. The Eagle Cap Wilderness in the Wallowas was one of the first pieces of Forest Reserve Land to be managed for recreation. And the 1975 Hells Canyon National Recreation Area designation increased public recognition of the recreational, archaeological, and historical values of this remote stretch of the Snake River.

The Wallowa Valley was the summer home of the "Joseph band" of the Nez Perce Indians. They hunted and fished in the mountains, lakes, and streams, grazed ponies in the lush valleys, and wintered in the nearby canyons of the Snake and its tributaries. Chief Joseph and his band left the Wallowas in 1877, beginning a fighting retreat that became one of the last and most famous of the Indian Wars.

Today, this valley is the population center and "hub," as it were, of a scenic and recreation paradise. The area is very rural, the county seat of Enterprise (pop. 2020) being the largest town between La Grande, Oregon, 65 miles to the southwest, and Lewiston, Idaho, which is 85 miles to the north. The Wallowa Valley is reached from the south and west via Hwy. 82, which intersects with Interstate 84 in La Grande, and from the north and east via Hwy. 3 (Washington Hwy 129) which leaves Clarkston, Washington near U.S. Hwy 95.

Wallowa County harbors a magnificent array of flora, fauna, and geological phenomenon. Elevations range from under 1,000 feet above sea level at the lower Snake River area to 9,845 feet at Matterhorn Peak in the Wallowa Mountains. Forests of pine, fir, larch, and spruce are interspersed with other conifers and deciduous species throughout the county. Deer, elk, bighorn sheep, cougar, bear, and a wonderful variety of smaller animals, birds, and fishes are abundant.

HIKING THE HIGH WALLOWAS AND HELLS CANYON attempts to be representative rather than comprehensive. The trail information, bibliography, and maps are meant to help you get started on your own hiking experience—your own kinds of discoveries.

All of the hikes covered in the book are through public lands or right of ways managed by the U.S. Forest Service. Some are appropriate for horse travel. Others touch areas that can also be reached by river boat or raft. Guide and packing services are available through a number of professional outfitters operating out of the valley.

Maps in the book are all based on the latest USFS contour maps with two exceptions. Because of their lengths, the maps for hikes #4 and #18 are based on U.S. Forest Service 1/2-mile maps. Of necessity, the maps in the book cover only the immediate area of the designated hikes. You can buy the Eagle Cap Wilderness map, the Hells Canyon NRA map, and the Wenaha-Tucannon Wilderness map at local USFS offices and at many area stores. There is also an excellent USFS map of the Wallowa-Whitman National Forest which covers all of Wallowa County and virtually everything covered in this book. The one exception is a bit of the Wenaha River trail. The Bookloft and the Hells Canyon NRA visitor's center in Enterprise, The Sports Corral in Joseph, and the Matterhorn Swiss Village at Wallowa Lake all carry USGS topographical maps.

Unless otherwise noted, all maps in the book point north to the top of the page. The letters in parentheses in the text of each hike refer to the letters on the map of that hike. The distances given for each hike will vary slightly from map to map and hiker to hiker. Trails are occasionally rerouted to accommodate a windfall or rockslide. Distances given are from the best information available at the time of publication.

Water is available on most hikes but should be boiled or treated before drinking. Insects are most abundant during summer months at elevations over 6,000 feet. Poison ivy along lower elevations of the Snake, Imnaha, and Grande Ronde rivers is far more dangerous than snakes or bears.

The weather, road and trail conditions change drastically in Wallowa County during the year—sometimes within days.

Be sure to ask locally about conditions before hiking. Many local residents are outdoor oriented and can give you information. If they don't know, they know someone who does! Ask at USFS offices and at outdoor stores, at the Imnaha Store and Tavern in Imnaha and at the Bookloft in Enterprise. The Bookloft also carries field guides appropriate to the area.

It is important to realize that most of the hikes described in this book (with the major exception of Hike #12 in the Lakes Basin) take place in areas that are very sparsely populated. It is not uncommon to hike an entire trail and not see another person. If this fact disturbs you, be sure to take the necessary precautions and let people know where you are going. Also—fire has played a major role in NE Oregon forests during the last decade. Check with USFS offices for the latest information on trails and hikes affected by fire.

As you travel, be aware of Wilderness designations. Wilderness boundaries are clearly marked along the trails and Wilderness use regulations are posted at trailheads. Motorized and mechanized vehicles and equipment (including bicycles) are not allowed in Wilderness areas. Permits are required in the Eagle Cap Wilderness beginning in 1995. The permits, to monitor use, are free and available at trailheads and USFS offices. The maximum party size for the Eagle Cap Wilderness is currently 12. In the Lakes Basin, the maximum party size for overnight camping is six. These regulations are subject to change, so inquire as to present rules.

We urge you to help keep Wilderness areas special. Camp away from lakes to keep water pure. Hobble, picket, or hitchline stock (rather than tying them to trees) to prevent damage to trees. Pick up a candy wrapper or cigarette butt and take apart a fire ring. Look at, enjoy, photograph, but do not pick up and pack off fossils, artifacts, or other natural and/or fuel resources. Be sensitive to the Wilderness and to others using it as you travel.

Finally, Wallowa County has more Wilderness area than any other county in Oregon, and some geologists have suggested that the entire area be designated a national geological park because of its unique physical features. These things bother some local loggers and ranchers. And the economic backbone of Wallowa County is logging and ranching—which disturbs some hikers, hunters, and fishermen. And of course there are some community leaders who would like to subordinate all of the above to tourism development on the scale of a Yosemite or a Sun Valley.

Because of geography, weather, altitude, etc., Wallowa County will likely continue to change at its own slow pace, and will continue to have a rich diversity of people and ideas. When you visit and hike, you might meet ranchers, hunters, cows, logging trucks, pack trains, fishermen, and tourists—to name a few. And you will find that most of the people you meet will be friendly and interesting. You may not share their philosophies, but take some time to share ideas. The people are as interesting as the scenery. After all, this is a place where a person can find the time and the space to think beyond the tip of his or her nose. Good hiking!

Standley Guard Station. (Dave Jensen photo)

1 BEAR CREEK/DOBBIN CREEK/STANDLEY SPRING

FOREST SERVICE TRAIL NOS. 1653, 1654

SEASONAL ACCESS: Late spring, summer and fall. This trail opens early on its lower part due to less snow and lower elevation.

ELEVATION: 4,000'—7,200'

DIRECTIONS TO TRAILHEAD: Bear Creek Trailhead (A) is located 9 miles south of Wallowa at Boundary Campground. Turn off Highway 82 at Goebel's Texaco on the west end of Wallowa and go west on First St. for 0.4 miles. Turn left on Bear Creek Rd. Follow this winding road for about 8 miles to its end at Boundary Campground. The road is paved for its first 2 miles, becomes USFS Road 8250 at the national forest boundary, and finally USFS Road 040 for the last mile before the trailhead.

TRAILHEAD SPECIFICS: The campground at the trailhead offers a dozen sites with picnic tables, fire rings and pit toilets. Water from Bear Creek should be boiled before drinking. Stock facilities at the trailhead include a loading ramp and hitching rails.

TRAIL DISTANCE: The distance from the trailhead to Standley Trail junction is 4.5 miles. From this junction on Bear Creek to Standley Spring is 4.7 miles. Total round trip distance is 18.4 miles.

TRAIL CHARACTER: The trail along Bear Creek is gentle with no major side streams until Goat Creek (4.0 miles) where a foot/stock bridge (B) is located. The trail up to Dobbin Creek and Standley crosses Bear Creek and the crossing can be difficult during the spring runoff, but other times it is usually less than knee deep. From Bear Creek to Standley Spring (C) the trail rises 2,600' in less than 5 miles. It is graded with switchbacks with no overly steep sections.

LANDMARKS AND POINTS OF INTEREST: The first 4.5 miles of trail follow Bear Creek through stands of fir, larch and pine. After the spring runoff there are many good fishing holes that will yield Rainbow, Brook, and Dolly Varden trout. Along the way the Swainson's Thrush (one of the fine singing thrushes) will often be heard, but seldom seen, hidden in the tree branches.

A bridge crosses Goat Creek 4 miles up the trail. A well-used campsite is located here. An old Forest Service cabin is located on the right side of the trail about 0.3 miles past the bridge. Another campsite is located 0.5 miles past the bridge at the junction of the Dobbin Creek Trail.

The Dobbin Creek Trail angles up the west slope of the valley wall for the next mile before reaching Dobbin Creek and the beginning of a steeper ascent. The shade of the spruce/fir forest is welcome for the rest of the climb. The trail levels out as the forest thins and a small, swampy meadow is found just before reaching the ridge saddle (just over 8 miles).

The junction with the Bear Wallow Trail is located on the ridge and the traveler turns left to follow the ridge another 0.7 miles to Standley Spring. A Forest Service cabin is located here that was built in 1932. The area was the site of early range studies that took place between 1907-1911.

A pipe with faucet is located at the spring. A campsite in the trees above and to the east of the spring offers shelter and a fire ring.

RECREATION: Fishing is good in Bear Creek from June until the season closes, usually on October 31.

Elk, deer, bighorn sheep and black bear are found in the area and it is a favorite of hunters. Archery season usually begins the latter part of August and many campsites are occupied by hunters until late November.

There is the potential for a long circle hike in the area if one goes south along Standley Ridge and then east back to Bear Creek. A trail was previously located along Miner Basin Creek, but is no longer maintained.

A day can be well spent wandering along the ridge and enjoying the splendid view. To the east, Bear Creek Canyon's rugged cliffs and ridges are a contrast to the wide, wooded valley of the Minam River to the west.

Far to the south and east, the tops of the Matterhorn and Eagle Cap peaks may be seen on a clear day.

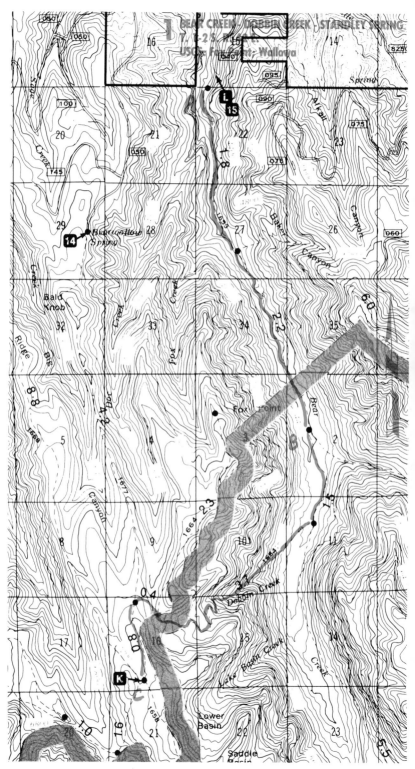

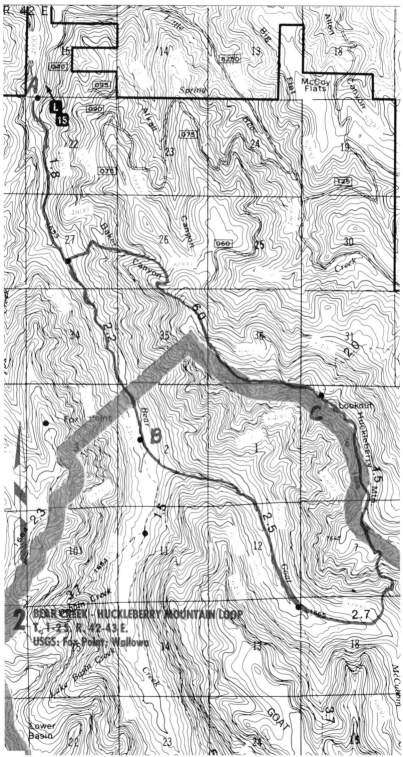

2 **BEAR CREEK - HUCKLEBERRY MOUNTAIN LOOP**
T. 1-2 S. R. 42-43 E.
USGS: Fox Point, Wallowa

2   BEAR CREEK/HUCKLEBERRY MOUNTAIN LOOP

FOREST SERVICE TRAIL NOS. 1653, 1665, 1667

SEASONAL ACCESS: Late spring, summer, and fall. The upper reaches of Huckleberry Mountain are snowbound usually into late June, but a clever eye can generally find the path earlier, even during May, depending on the severity of the previous winter's snowfall.

ELEVATION: 3,700'—7,700'

DIRECTION TO TRAILHEAD: See Hike #1

TRAILHEAD SPECIFICS: See Hike #1

TRAIL DISTANCE: The trail distance from the trailhead to Goat Creek (B) is 4.0 miles. From Goat Creek to the old lookout site on top of Huckleberry Mountain is 6.7 miles. From Huckleberry Mountain (C) down Baker Canyon to Trail No. 1653 is 6.0 miles. Two miles down Trail No. 1653 takes you back to the trailhead. The entire loop is a distance of just over 18 miles.

TRAIL CHARACTER: The entire trail can be easily hiked without any technical knowledge; there are no large or difficult stream crossings. The mean elevation of the hike is about 4,500'—3,700' at the trailhead up to 7,700' on the summit of Huckleberry Mountain.

LANDMARKS AND POINTS OF INTEREST: Trail No. 1653 proceeds up Bear Creek (which is closer to being a small river than a large creek) on its northward journey from the midst of the Wallowa Mountains. After 4 miles of relatively easy hiking along a stretch of trail which skirts an area generally offering a wide array of wildflowers in the upland meadows, the river valley widens, and the junction with Goat Creek Trail No. 1665 is clearly visible.

The climb up Goat Creek is relatively steep, but views of McCubbin Basin to the southeast quench the weariness. Three miles up Goat Creek (don't forget to fill your water skins here) the trail leaves the creek and begins a switchbacking ascent up the south face of Huckleberry Mountain. If you decide you can't make it all the way up, the best camping spots are in the area where the switchbacks climb midst pleasant meadows containing a riot of colorful wildflowers.

The summit of Huckleberry Mountain offers magnificent vistas in every direction. The view north to the Wallowa Valley and beyond to the forested ridges of the Powwatka country is particularly impressive.

The summit of Huckleberry—which is actually a long ridge running mostly northwest to southeast—also offers the possibility of meeting, or encountering, or confronting, depending upon the manner of your approach, one of the peculiar cinnamon-colored black bear that frequent this area in the summer months.

Following the ridge of Huckleberry Mountain, you will eventually come to a trail which branches off and descends the north face of the mountain. Do not take this trail. It is Trail No. 1665 and descends 2 miles to a trailhead on USFS Road 8250. Stay on Trail No. 1667 which continues northwesterly for about 2 miles along the ridge and then descends steeply downhill toward Baker Gulch. It is possible to lose the trail when it passes through clearings in Baker Gulch. If that happens, do not worry. The main Bear Creek trail is always below—continue heading down the gulch.

The trail eventually intersects with Trail No. 1653 less than 2 miles from the trailhead where this loop hike originated. A hardy soul could make the loop in a day, but some might prefer to camp in the aforementioned area near the switchback on the south face of Huckleberry Mountain.

RECREATION: This is an excellent loop trail since one never retraces steps until the last 1.5 miles. The scenery is diverse—mostly alpine type landscape and glacially-carved granite. The route is classic: up a river, up a snowborn mountain creek, up and across a mountain, and down a wooded gulch.

Much of the route is inside, or adjacent to, the Eagle Cap Wilderness. This part of the wilderness is not heavily used and it is not uncommon to hike the entire loop and never see another person. The area is more heavily used during the hunting seasons in late summer and fall.

3 HUCKLEBERRY MOUNTAIN

FOREST SERVICE TRAIL NO. 1665

SEASONAL ACCESS: From snowmelt to snowfall—usually May through November.

ELEVATION: 5,600'—7,600'

DIRECTIONS TO TRAILHEAD: Turn west off Highway 82 at Goebel's Texaco station in Wallowa onto First St. At 0.4 miles turn left onto a paved road that is signed Bear Creek Rd. Follow this winding road for 7.2 miles—it turns to dirt after 2.1 miles. At 7.2 miles turn left on a gravel road labeled "Huckleberry Trail—7 miles." This is USFS Road 8250. Go up this road exactly 7.2 miles from the above junction. The trailhead parking area is not marked but is a right turn at 7.2 miles. The turn occurs after the road you're on comes over a rise and starts going down. The road is barely passable to cars—a truck or 4X4 vehicle is recommended.

TRAILHEAD SPECIFICS: The trailhead, once you find the turn-out, is fairly obvious as it is also used as a stock driveway. There is ample parking. No stock unloading ramp is present. No water is available. The trailhead is marked only with a USFS trail regulation sign.

TRAIL DISTANCE: From the trailhead (A) to the top of Huckleberry Mountain (B) is 2 miles. The trail then connects with other trails.

TRAIL CHARACTER: This trail, though short, is fairly steep. The trailhead is at approximately 5,600' and the elevation at the old fire lookout is approximately 7,600', giving an elevation gain of 2,000' in 2 miles. The trail is in good condition; however, it is extremely dusty when dry and extremely slippery when wet. Loose gravel on the steep pitches provides very unstable footing in all weather so watch your step! The only water available on the trail is at 0.25 miles above the trailhead, where the trail crosses Little Bear Creek and at about 1.75 miles where a spring forms a boggy spot beside the trail. Early in the hiking season snowmelt may run down parts of the trail. All standard cautions to drinking this water apply. The crossing of Little Bear Creek is quite easy, although early summer snowmelt might make rock-hopping a bit more of a challenge.

LANDMARKS AND POINTS OF INTEREST: The trail starts in a second-growth Lodgepole Pine stand that quickly yields to a mixed conifer, unlogged forest. After crossing Little Bear Creek the trail leads steadily up, switchbacking across the northeast face of Huckleberry Mountain. The hiker is treated to many expansive views to the north: the Wallowa Valley, the Whiskey Creek hill country, and the north end of the Wallowa-Whitman National Forest. As you climb higher you especially notice the number of ranches scattered out in the hills above the valley floor. Reaching the boggy area 1.75 miles up the trail is a cool break on a hot day. Many interesting wildflowers that cannot be found on the surrounding slopes have grown up around this spring. Another 200 yards brings you to the wilderness boundary sign, and 200 yards beyond the sign you top out on the bare, windblown, broad summit of Huckleberry Mountain. The fire lookout that once topped the peak has been dismantled, and only a few piles of rock mark its former location.

RECREATION: Don't forget to bring your camera on this hike. From the mountaintop you get sweeping vistas in every direction—the Wallowa Valley to the east and the Eagle Cap Wilderness to the west and south. Once on top of Huckleberry mountain, you can hike the ridges to the northwest or southeast, on or off the trail. You walk through open dry meadows interspersed with small islands of trees. It's dry up here, however, so unless you plan to hike an additional 6.5 miles southeast to Little Storm Lake, carry lots of water and don't bother to bring a fishing pole. You have a limitless choice of campsites with a view from the top of the ridge.

COMMENTS: Although the drive to the trailhead over a rough and dusty road seems to take a long time and the trail is pretty steep in places, this is a nice day hike in the lower valley that gets you up into the wilderness area quickly. You are treated to great views all the way up as you stop to catch your breath. The wonderful views from on top plus the many places that beckon you to come exploring "just a little bit further" make it hard to leave at the end of the day. Solitude is another bonus of this trip—meeting other people on the trail is the exception rather than the rule.

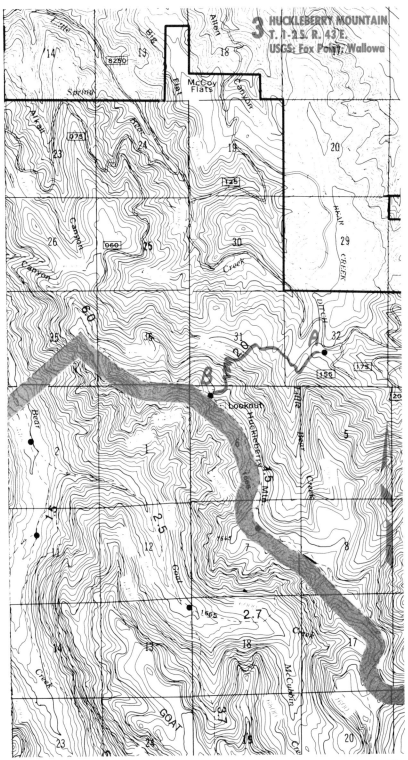

4   WENAHA RIVER — ELK FLAT

The two trailheads provide two accesses to the Wenaha River. They merge, and can be hiked trailhead to trailhead.

FOREST SERVICE TRAIL NOS. 3106—Wenaha, 3241—Elk Flat, 6144—Wenaha (sometimes designated "South Fork Wenaha")

SEASONAL ACCESS: The lower Wenaha River system can be accessed year around. The Elk Flat Trail and access to the trailhead is usually open May to November.

ELEVATION: Troy—1,600' to Elk Flat—5,000"

DIRECTIONS TO TRAILHEAD: From Enterprise, take Hwy. 3 north for 34 miles and turn left on a paved road to Flora and Troy. Stay on this road for 16 miles to Troy. The first 7 miles after turning off the main highway is paved and the rest is good gravel which is plowed daily in the winter in case of any snow.

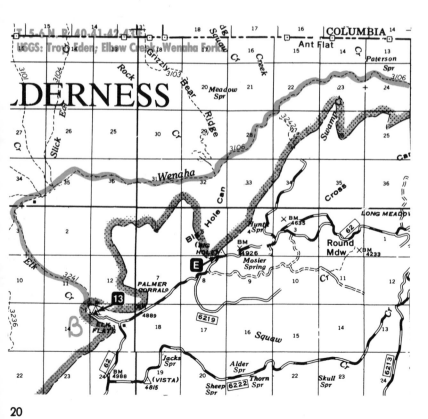

Locate Trail 3106 by driving from downtown Troy on the paved road, north, down the Grande Ronde River. After a couple of blocks a gravel road leads up the hill to the left with a sign pointing to Pomeroy. Take this road for 0.4 miles to the first right-hand switchback. The trailhead (A) starts here with a sign which shows distances to wilderness boundary (6) and the Wenaha Forks (21).

The trailhead (B) for Elk Flat Trail No. 3241 is reached as follows: from Troy, cross the bridge over the Wenaha River and go up the Grande Ronde River about 0.25 miles where the gravel road splits. Take the right fork, USFS Road 62, and proceed for 21 miles. Turn right on Road 290 and go 0.75 miles to the Elk Flat Trailhead. There is a good sign on Road 62 designating the turnoff to the trailhead.

Traveling from Troy on Road 62 there are several other important mileage points. Long Meadows is 12.7 miles from Troy, the turnoff to Hoodoo Trailhead is 13.3 miles from Troy (the trailhead for Trail No. 3244—Hoodoo is 4.1 miles off Road 62), and the turnoff for the road to Cross Canyon Trailhead is 17 miles from Troy.

TRAILHEAD SPECIFICS: At the Wenaha River Trailhead No. 3106 there is parking for two or three cars. There are no

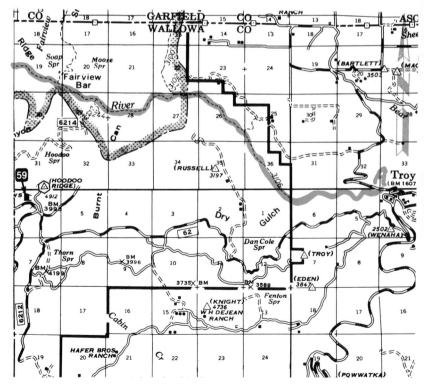

other facilities. The trail is obvious and signed with mileages marked from the trailhead.

The trailhead at Elk Flat for Trail No. 3241 has a stock loading ramp, toilets, picnic tables, and unlimited parking. There is no water. The trail is well signed and obvious. The trailhead has heavy use in summer and fall during hunting season.

TRAIL DISTANCE: For the first 9.1 miles from the Wenaha Trailhead, the river trail is designated No. 3106. At that point Trail No. 6144 merges from the north, and the river trail becomes No. 6144 and continues as such to the forks. One can hike or ride in from the Wenaha Trailhead on a one day jaunt or a multi-day fishing expedition. The trip to the forks is 21.1 miles one-way.

From the trailhead at Elk Flat to the south fork of the Wenaha is 5.0 miles on Trail No. 3241. You can hike to the forks and back in a day, but remember that the 1,800 feet of elevation lost must be regained. If you continue on No. 3241, it intersects with No. 6144 and you are on the main river trail. As an option to retracing your steps, you can come out of the Wenaha Canyon to Cross Canyon Trailhead at 6.9 miles from the forks (C), travel an additional 6.1 miles and exit to Hoodoo Trailhead (D), or hike the entire 27 miles from the Elk Flat Trailhead to the Wenaha Trailhead (A). All of these options require an extra vehicle or a shuttle arrangement.

TRAIL CHARACTER: Wenaha Trail No. 3106 has a gentle grade, stream water is available, and the trail is well maintained. The trail stays on the north side of the river for its entire length so there are no river crossings, however stream crossings may be difficult during the runoff months of April, May and June.

The Elk Flat Trail No. 3241 drops 1,800' in 5 miles. The trail is well maintained and well signed. There is no water until the south fork is reached. There are good crossings for the south fork and on side streams- however the north fork of the Wenaha must be forded to reach Trail No. 3106 and this can pose some difficulty for hikers if the water is high.

LANDMARKS AND POINTS OF INTEREST: Vegetation along the lower Wenaha River changes from open grassland rimrock to very dense riparian vegetation and finally to forests.

Numerous trails intersect the Wenaha Trail including Crooked Fork No. 3100, Hoodoo Springs No. 3244, Smooth Ridge No. 6144, Cross Canyon No. 3242, Rock Creek No.

3103, and Trapper Ridge No. 3235. The South Fork Trail No. 6144 goes 10.2 miles to Timothy Springs Guard Station which is located on Road 6415.

The Wenaha Canyon is basalt type with vegetation typical of the Blue Mountain Range. Crooked Creek, Rock Creek, Butte Creek, Beaver Creek, and the North Fork are major tributaries to the Wenaha along Trail No. 3106.

RECREATION: The Wenaha River is managed for wild fish. Rainbow and Dolly Varden are abundant, and salmon spawn in the river. Mule Deer, Whitetail Deer, elk, black bear, and grouse are abundant. The area receives its heaviest use during the hunting seasons. Primitive campsites are found all along the river. The area is a wonderful place to explore because access is difficult and limited. The Wenaha-Tucannon Wilderness is truly an area where one can escape man and man's activities.

COMMENTS: The Wenaha River provides visitors an opportunity to see a major stream generally unaffected by man's activity. Waters run cold and clear — fish, otter, and raccoon abound. So do rattlesnakes!

Wenaha River. (Dave Jensen photo)

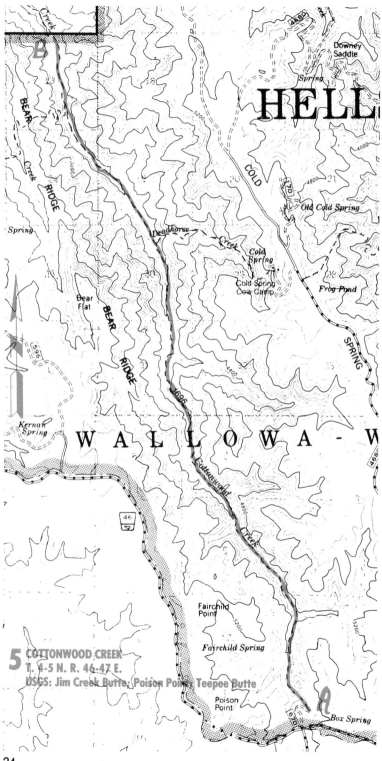

B

Creek

Downey
Saddle

4680

Spring

HELL

BEAR

COLD

4800

Creek

170

Old Cold Spring

RIDGE

Spring

Deadhorse Creek

Cold
Spring

Bear
Flat

Cold Spring
Cow Camp

Frog Pond

BEAR

RIDGE

SPRING

4100

596

4800

Kernan
Spring

W A L L O W A - W

46

4680

Cottonwood Creek

Fairchild
Point

5200

Fairchild Spring

5 COTTONWOOD CREEK
T. 4-5 N. R. 46-47 E.
USGS: Jim Creek Butte; Poison Point; Teepee Butte

Poison
Point

670

A

Box Spring

24

5 COTTONWOOD CREEK

FOREST SERVICE TRAIL NO. 1696

SEASONAL ACCESS: Late spring through late fall.

ELEVATION: 2,760' — 5,140'

DIRECTIONS TO TRAILHEAD: From Enterprise go southeast toward Joseph on Hwy. 82 for about 3 miles. Turn left at the sign for Buckhorn Springs. At 1.4 miles on this paved road there will be a junction with the Swamp Creek Road coming in from the north. Pass this junction and stay on what is now the Crow Creek Road heading east for another 3.9 miles. At the fork in the road take a right, onto the Zumwalt Road (USFS 46). The road is improved and easy to follow. You will stay on this road for 41.8 miles at which point there is a four-way intersection with USFS Road 4625 and Vigne Campground to the left (south) and USFS Road 4600-670 and the NRA boundary to the right (north). Go right for 0.3 miles. The Cottonwood Creek Trailhead is signed on a tree about 50 yards below the road switchback.

See ending comments for description of a brief side-trip off USFS Road 46 which is indeed worthwhile!

TRAILHEAD SPECIFICS: The trailhead sign (A) is not outwardly obvious and a few people have claimed that they did not see it. With the above directions, it should be easy to find.

If logging or other heavy road traffic is taking place, the trailhead may not be a good place to park. A spur road is located 0.2 miles further and ends 0.9 miles from the trailhead. This would be a good place to park.

There are no loading ramps in the vicinity of the trailhead. Some roadcuts or sidehills may be usable instead.

The nearest water is in Cottonwood Creek and is probably most potable about 0.5 miles down the trail where a couple of side drainages enter — although flowing water is present above that point.

TRAIL DISTANCE: From the trailhead to the forest boundary is approximately 10 miles one-way.

TRAIL CHARACTER: Trail condition is intermittently good-poor-nonexistent! There are several unmarked forks, a few of which do not reconnect with the main trail. The entire area was burned in 1988 by the Teepee Butte fire. Resulting snags easily blow down across the trail. Be sure to check at USFS offices for latest trail information. The lower section of the trail is relatively open and less subject to blowdowns.

Water is available in the creek except where it subs a couple of times for short distances in the midsummer.

Total elevation loss from the trailhead to the forest boundary (B) is 2,380'. Overall, the trail follows easy contours.

There are numerous stream crossings. In spring, you'll get your feet wet.

LANDMARKS AND POINTS OF INTEREST: From top to bottom, this trail leads through three major vegetation zones and the ecotones between them. Uppermost in elevation, Englemann Spruce (Picea englemannii) is dominant. Tree species become more mixed within two miles of the trailhead. Fire affected many trees, but keep your eyes open for the very large old growth Douglas and Grand Fir (Pseudotsuga menziesii, Abies grandis), Western Larch (Larix occidentalis) and Ponderosa Pine (Pinus ponderosa) which survived. After the fire, grasses and shrubs sprang up as sunlight increased and the flora diversified. In the lower third of this trail, at and below Smooth Gulch, the canyon widens and the huge pine dominate.

Mazama ash, upturned by burrowing mammals or exposed in layers by spring runoff, is visible intermittently along the trail. This fine, light-colored soil was deposited by the eruption of Mt. Mazama (Crater Lake) 6,000 years ago and contributes to the fertile conditions which support the dense vegetation in this canyon.

Exploring along several stretches of this trail would best be done within your physical limitations! The canyon walls are frequently steep and brushy. Below Smooth Gulch, side canyons are wider and quite enticing.

RECREATION: "Really nice" campsites, for hunting or even just for a hiker's night or two, are hard to find anywhere above Smooth Gulch. Above that point, the canyon is pretty steep and narrow and the ground is usually sloping.

The creek is choked periodically by logs and other fallen debris; however, there are some small trout there.

This is post-fire country and the game and non-game wildlife associated with this habitat is likely to be found here. Several species of woodpeckers and both Western and Mountain Bluebirds highly utilize the snags.

It is possible to have a vehicle drop you off at the trailhead and then pick you up on the lower reaches of Cottonwood Creek. This is a 15-18 mile hike depending on how far up Cottonwood Creek the vehicle can travel (be sure to check this item before you start hiking).

COMMENTS: The brief side trip mentioned earlier is as follows: take USFS Road 46 32.6 miles from its junction with Crow Creek Road. Turn off to the right of USFS Road 780 and go 0.75 miles to the Buckhorn Observation Point. The view is magnificent—and only 1.5 miles out of the way to the trailhead.

The country you will be driving through along USFS Road 46, the Zumwalt Prairie, supports the nation's highest density of nesting Ferruginous Hawks (*Buteo regalis*) as well as many other raptors.

Prior to hunting seasons in the fall, the solitude of this area is one of its outstanding features. You are not likely to meet anyone else hiking on Cottonwood Creek Trail.

Smooth Gulch off lower Cottonwood Trail (Laurel Reuben photo)

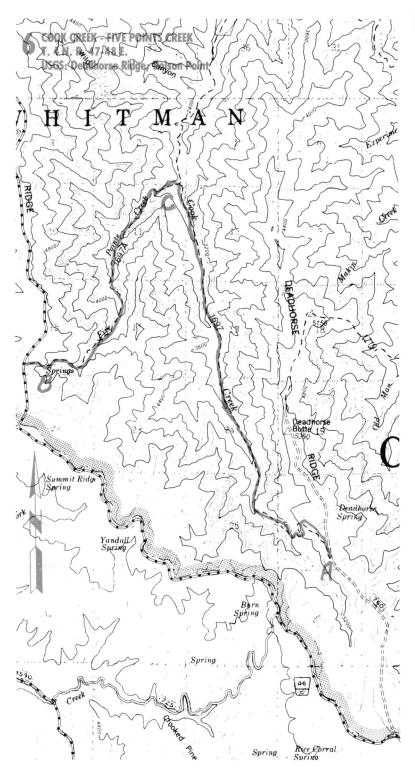

W H I T M A N

Springs

Summit Ridge
Spring

Yandall
Spring

Byrn
Spring

Spring

Deadhorse
Butte

Deadhorse
Spring

C

DEADHORSE RIDGE

Rice Corral
Spring

Crooked Pine

28

6 COOK CREEK/FIVE POINTS CREEK

These trails can be hiked as two separate hikes or, with some preparation, as one hike. In the first case, one begins at either the Cook Creek or the Five Points Trailhead, hikes to the fork of the two streams, and returns by the same route to trailhead and vehicle. Alternatively, with some pre-planning and an extra vehicle or a shuttle arrangement, one can begin at one trailhead and come out at the other.

FOREST SERVICE TRAIL NOS. 1697, 1697A

SEASONAL ACCESS: May to November — there are snow drifts on the ridge roads in the early spring. USFS Road 760 is also closed some years after October 1 due to deer and elk hunting restrictions.

ELEVATION: 3,000' — 5,100'

DIRECTIONS TO TRAILHEAD: See Hike #5. Once you reach the junction of Crow Creek and Zumwalt roads, turn right on Zumwalt Road (USFS 46) and proceed 32 miles to Deadhorse Ridge Road (USFS 760). Turn right and stay on USFS Road 760 for two miles — on the left you will see the trailhead cairn for Cook Creek Trail.
   The Five Points Creek Trailhead is reached as above except do not turn off USFS 46 onto USFS 760. Continue another 6.0 miles on USFS Road 46 and turn right on USFS Road 4680 (Cold Springs Road). Proceed 0.8 miles to the trailhead on the righthand side of the road.

TRAILHEAD SPECIFICS: From Cook Creek Trailhead on Deadhorse Ridge (A) there is no water until you reach the bottom of the canyon (about 2 miles). The only improvement at the trailhead is a rock cairn with a sign. The trail from the cairn is not obvious. When standing directly in front of the cairn, estimate where one o'clock would be and walk in this direction. After 200 yards there will be a small rock cairn and the trail becomes more obvious.
   There is a sign on a tree at Five Points Creek Trailhead (B). There are no other improvements. Water is available only when the trail hits Five Points Creek (about 0.8 miles). There is an old Forest Service sign about 0.25 miles from the trailhead where the trail goes through an opening and begins to drop down to Five Points Creek. There is room for parking at either trailhead.

TRAIL DISTANCE: It is about 6 miles from the Cook Creek Trailhead to the junction of Cook Creek and Five Points Creek (C). From this junction to the Five Points Creek Trailhead is 4 miles.

TRAIL CHARACTER: There are only a few stream crossings on the Cook Creek Trail and they pose no problem except for a couple of weeks in the early spring during snowmelt. Five Points Creek Trail has more stream crossings but the streams are much smaller. Waterproof footwear during the spring runoff would be advisable.

The Five Points Creek Trail is quite steep—dropping 2,000' in 4 miles. Cook Creek Trail has the same elevation drop but it is over a longer distance, making for a slightly easier descent and ascent. Neither trail is heavily used. The Tee-pee Butte fire burned this area in 1988 and the same conditions apply as described in Hike #5. The trail is usually cleared, but it would be wise to check at the Hells Canyon NRA office in Enterprise on the current status of trailhead markings and trail conditions.

LANDMARKS AND POINTS OF INTEREST: From the trailhead on Cook Creek the trail gently descends the east slope of the canyon. After a few switchbacks the trail ties into an old logging road. A large rock cairn was built at this point so the trail could be found when coming up the old logging road from the opposite direction. Following the old road to its end, it again turns into a trail and continues down the east side of Cook Creek to the junction with Five Points Creek.

Five Points Creek Trail follows down a narrow canyon where patches of Douglas Fir, Tamarack, White Fir, and Ponderosa Pine remain untouched by the fire. Where fire burned, sunlight has brought on a profusion of grasses, alder, and other shrubs among blackened snags. Among the remaining thickets, it is cool in the summer and very protected in the winter. A feeling of isolation becomes a reality here, but it is a calm feeling of being in an untouched forest in a deep canyon.

RECREATION: The best area for camping is at the forks of Cook Creek and Five Points Creek. There is fishing here for small Red-banded Trout. This unique relative of the Rainbow Trout is native to only a few tributaries of the Snake River in this area. Rocky Mt. elk, mule deer, and black bear are fairly common in the area. Blue grouse and chukar inhabit the open ridges and pileated woodpeckers are found in the old growth forest remnants along the stream.

If one is camped at the junction of Cook Creek and Five Points Creek, there are options of hiking down Cook Creek and taking side trips on Cherry Creek Trail (USFS No. 1705) or up Downey Gulch. Hiking Trail No. 1705 gives excellent views into Hells Canyon and toward the mouth of the Salmon River.

COMMENTS: Many people have discovered that of all the outstanding natural features of Wallowa County, their favorites are the deep canyons leading down to numerous river drainages. Descending into the canyon depths and exploring their walls can lead to a feeling of wonderment and excitement.

A stand of Ponderosa Pine on the Five Points Trail near Cook Creek. Notice old fire scar on tree to left. Fire again went through the stand in 1988. (Mike Bohannon photo)

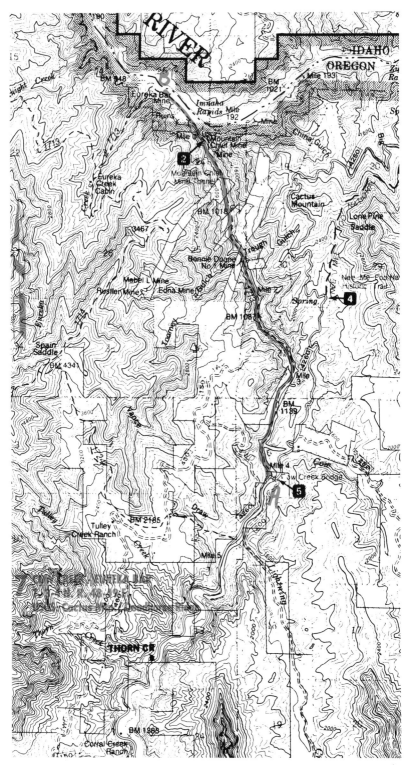

7 COW CREEK—EUREKA BAR

FOREST SERVICE TRAIL NO. 1713

SEASONAL ACCESS: All year.

ELEVATION: 900'—1,100'

DIRECTIONS TO TRAILHEAD: From Joseph take Hwy. 350 east to Imnaha (31 miles). In Imnaha turn left and follow the paved road down the Imnaha River. The sign at the intersection points to "Lower Imnaha." The road is paved for about 6 miles to Fence Creek where the graveled portion begins and the road becomes USFS 4260. From this point it is approximately 20 miles to the trailhead (A) at Cow Creek bridge. The trailhead is very well marked, however, and it is at this point that USFS Road 4260 leaves the Imnaha River and heads over Cactus Mt. to Dug Bar.

TRAILHEAD SPECIFICS: The trailhead is located on the left side of Road 4260 just before the road crosses the Imnaha River at Cow Creek bridge (the bridge crosses the Imnaha—not Cow Creek). There are a couple of signs at the trailhead designating the trail to Eureka Bar.

There are a few primitive campsites at the trailhead, parking is available, water is plentiful but must be boiled, and there is a great swimming hole in the Imnaha River downstream from the bridge. There is a stock unloading ramp and pit toilets.

TRAIL DISTANCE: It is about 4.2 miles from the trailhead to the mouth of the Imnaha River on the Snake River. Eureka Bar (B) is another 0.7 miles downstream from the mouth of the Imnaha. The 10 mile round trip makes for an easy day hike with plenty of time left for fishing or exploring.

TRAIL CHARACTER: The trail is river grade the entire length with a gradual decline to the Snake River. The trail follows the west side of the Imnaha River and there are no stream or river crossings. Since the trail is close to the river at some points there may be rare occasions during early spring runoff when high water covers small stretches of the trail with a few inches of water. The only water available on the trail is from the river. Pay attention to poison ivy which is abundant along the trail and the river.

Hay fever sufferers should take precautions during May and June when the lush sweet clover is in bloom along the trail.

LANDMARKS AND POINTS OF INTEREST: The character of the trail remains constant throughout the 4 miles. A power line crosses high above the trail about one-third of the way to the Snake River and an old 3-mile marker is attached to a boulder on the left side of the trail. When the trail reaches the mouth of the Imnaha and turns left, the old foundations of the Eureka smelter can be seen. Around the turn of the century there was a thriving small town built around the smelter and the surrounding mines. **(SNAKE RIVER OF HELLS CANYON** — Backeddy Books — gives an excellent account of mining and steamboating along this section of the Snake River.) One old mine shaft and tracks can be seen across the Imnaha River before the Imnaha runs into the Snake — the shaft running through to the other side of the ridge and opening up on the Snake River.

In spring and early summer, many wildflowers line the trail. Many, such as the Prickly Pear Cactus *(Opuntia)*, Blazing Star, and Primrose, are typical of high desert ecosystems. Western Fence Lizards inhabit the canyon as do the Great Basin Rattlesnakes.

The stamp mill at Eureka Bar. Only the stone foundations remain. (Idaho Historical Society photo)

RECREATION: Fishing is good in the Imnaha during the cooler parts of the year. The water becomes quite warm in summer and fishing deteriorates. Mule Deer and bighorn sheep may be seen from the trail, especially during the cooler months. The entire hike is worth the time to see the different species of wildlife — birds, reptiles, mammals, etc. It is possible to make a circle hike by continuing down Trail No. 1713 along the Snake River and then following up Eureka Creek, across the head of Toomey Gulch to Tulley Creek and then back down to the Imnaha River Road. A good map will show this route.

Young fisherman on lower Imnaha River near confluence with the Snake. (Rich Wandschneider photo)

8   FREEZEOUT — SADDLE CREEK

FOREST SERVICE TRAIL NO. 1776

SEASONAL ACCESS: Spring, summer, and fall. The trail-head on Freezeout Creek on the Imnaha side and the lower portion of the trail on Saddle Creek on the Snake River side are often open all year long. Freezeout Saddle usually is snowed in from late fall until early spring.

ELEVATION: 3,000' at the trailhead — 5,500' at Freezeout Saddle — 1,400' on the Snake River.

DIRECTIONS TO TRAILHEAD: Take State Hwy. 350 east from Joseph for 31 miles to Imnaha. In Imnaha turn right (south, up river) on the Upper Imnaha road. This road is a good all-weather gravel road. Follow this road up the Imnaha for 13 miles and turn left on USFS Road 4230 which leads to the trailhead. There is a sign at the intersection of the roads which reads: "Saddle Creek Trail 4 miles." The trailhead is at the end of this road.

TRAILHEAD SPECIFICS: At the trailhead there are toilets and a stock unloading ramp. Some parking is available. Water is available from nearby Freezeout Creek. No motorized vehicles are allowed beyond this point.

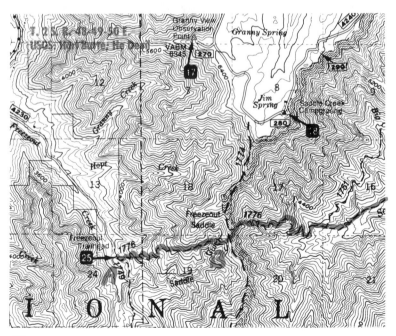

TRAIL DISTANCE: From the trailhead (A) to Freezeout Saddle (B) the distance is 2 miles. From Freezeout Saddle to the Snake River (C) is 9 miles. The total roundtrip distance is 22 miles.

TRAIL CHARACTER: The trail from the trailhead to Freezeout Saddle climbs 2,500' in 2 miles and is moderately steep. The trail is well maintained with no difficult stream crossings. The trail drops 4,000' in 9 miles on the descent from Freezeout Saddle to the Snake River. The grade is steep for the first 2 miles, and well maintained its entire length. Saddle Creek must be crossed several times. Crossings are not difficult and one can usually step on rocks or find a log.

LANDMARKS AND POINTS OF INTEREST: From the trailhead one reaches the junction of Trail No. 1749 in 0.25 miles. This trail takes off to the right and follows Freezeout Creek to the south. It is poorly maintained, but hikable. The Saddle Creek Trail continues to the left and begins to climb up through old growth pine and then into open, grassy terrain. From this point there is no more water along the trail until one crosses over the ridge and reaches Saddle Creek.

Grass species change as one climbs toward Freezeout Saddle. Bunch grass becomes dominant and showy wildflowers such as Arrowleaf Balsamroot, Penstemon, Flax, Sego Lily, and showy daisy bloom in the openings.

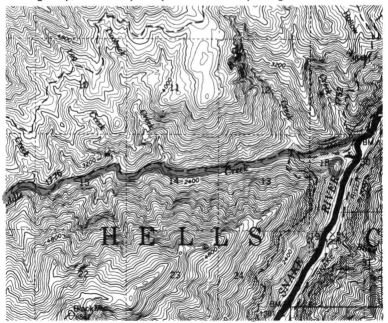

At Freezeout Saddle there is a rock cairn and there are signs at the intersection of Summit Trail No. 1774. This trail leads south to Marks Cabin and the head of Battle Creek; or north to the Hat Point Road and Memaloose. From the rock cairn the Saddle Creek Trail starts a steep descent down to the north side of Saddle Creek. At the bottom of this steep portion, the trail crosses the old stock driveway coming in from the north. This is also the High Trail No. 1751 which leads to Sluice Creek.

Following Saddle Creek down toward the Snake River, one passes through a burned-over region. The Freezeout fire occurred in August 1973, devastating old growth forest. In the spring one will find the beautiful golden-yellow Glacier Lily along the trail in moist areas. Wildlife found in the area include Mule Deer, cougar, elk, black bear, and Golden Eagle. As one descends to lower elevations, signs of ancient Indian sites can be observed.

About one mile before reaching the Snake River, Trail No. 1786 intersects on the right. There is a sign indicating mileage to the south to Cache Creek and Battle Creek. The Saddle Creek Trail continues down to the Snake River and then continues north down the Snake River to Sluice Creek and eventually Dug Bar. Devil's Slide, a section of the trail cut out of solid rock, is a short hike north on the trail and well worth the effort. Where Saddle Creek runs into the Snake River, there are signs of early irrigation projects, ranching, and building sites — although nothing remains today.

RECREATION: Campsites at the trailhead are primitive at best. There are many good places to camp on Freezeout Saddle (without water), and numerous sites along Saddle Creek. Several established campsites exist along the Snake River by the mouth of Saddle Creek.

Fishing for trout and bass in the Snake River can be very good in the spring and fall. Many rafters float the river in the summer but permits are required. Hunting season from August through November brings the heaviest use to the area, especially the trailhead. The potential for photography on this hike is outstanding.

COMMENTS: Access into the Snake River area for hikers, horse-people, etc. is very limited at present. The Freeze-out-Saddle Creek Trail is one of the least difficult ways to access the area. The startling differences in plant types and scenery due to changes in elevation are especially rewarding.

There are several great opportunities for loop hikes off the Saddle Creek Trail. One can hike down Saddle Creek to Trail No. 1786, up the Snake River to Battle Creek to Lookout Mt., and then back to the trailhead on Trail No. 1774 or Trail No. 1749. Another option is to hike down Saddle Creek and down the Snake River on Trail No. 1776 to Sluice Creek, up Sluice Creek on Trail No. 1748, and then along the High Trail No. 1751 back to the Saddle Creek Trail. Both hikes contain a great diversity of scenery. Freezeout Saddle in early spring may have deep snow but lower elevations will be open.

Bill George, shown here on Freezeout Saddle, began hiking in the Wallowa country at an age when most people retire from such activities. Bill is an avid photographer, outdoor enthusiast, and conservationist. Over the past 25 years he has introduced hundreds of people to remote sections of the Wallowas and Hells Canyon country and organized volunteer crews to clean up wilderness areas. (Janie Tippett photo)

9 IMNAHA RIVER

FOREST SERVICE TRAIL NO. 1816

SEASONAL ACCESS: June through October. Sometimes earlier or later depending on snow conditions.

ELEVATION: 4,600' — 5,400'

DIRECTIONS TO TRAILHEAD: From Joseph take the Imnaha Highway 350 east. Proceed past the 8 mile marker and take the first paved road to the right. It heads in a southerly direction with signs pointing to Halfway, Coverdale, and Lick Creek. Remain on this paved road for 17.8 miles until an intersection occurs. Take the right fork marked "Imnaha River — 14 miles." Go another 11.1 miles to a junction and remain on the right fork marked "Imnaha River — 2 miles" and "Halfway — 35 miles." Heed recommended speeds on this road since many curves are sharp for extended distances. From this junction go 11.1 miles to the trailhead at Indian Crossing. After the first 2 miles, a sign marked "Cloverdale — 5" and "Indian Crossing — 10" will reinforce your confidence. Do not cross the bridge at Ollokot Campground — continue up the right side of the Imnaha River to Indian Crossing. Six campgrounds are available along the Imnaha River.

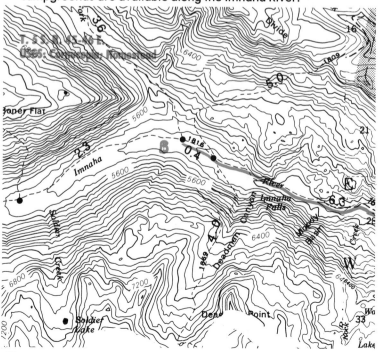

TRAILHEAD SPECIFICS: The trailhead is very obvious at the end of the road. There is a stock unloading ramp. Since the trailhead is located next to Indian Crossing campground, there is plenty of parking available and there are tables, water, toilets, and campsites.

TRAIL DISTANCE: The sign at the trailhead (A) indicates "North Fork Imnaha—9," "Cliff Creek—12," "Tenderfoot Pass—16," and "Hawkins Pass—18." The map shows the distance to the Imnaha Forks (B) at slightly less than 6 miles. With some bending and minimum switchbacks in rock formations, a short 7 miles is about right.

TRAIL CHARACTER: This is a well maintained trail with easy grades, gaining about 750' in elevation in 7 miles of distance. The middle stretch goes through and along rock formations and is less convenient to the river than the lower and upper sections. There are a few very short switchbacks in the rock formation areas. There are only a few very small streams to cross.

LANDMARKS AND POINTS OF INTEREST: Starting on the trail, a hiker passes a special use area with corrals and buildings. The Eagle Cap Wilderness boundary sign is about a mile up the trail.

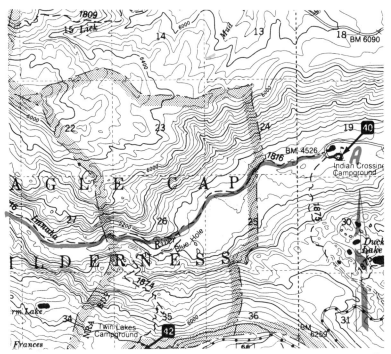

41

The "2 mile" marker is still in place. Immediately past the 2 mile marker the trail enters rock formations and is out of direct view of the river. A little exploring here and the hiker will find the river is a long deep hole running through sheer rock walls. This is the "Blue Hole."

At about 2.75 miles the trail goes by a small rock basin with an aspen patch as its principal vegetation — a delightful place to rest or picnic.

At about 3.25 miles the trail goes through a timber stand with a number of large larch and an understory of larch and Lodgepole Pine. For the remainder of the hike, large larch and an understory of Lodgepole Pine will be typical. This indicates a past fire that destroyed most trees, sparing only the large ones insulated by thick bark. The first section, with larch in the understory, didn't burn as hotly and conditions for regeneration were favorable to other species besides Lodgepole Pine.

At 4.0 miles two foot bridges are part of the trail. At 6.75 miles a trail from Lick Creek, No. 1809, joins the main trail. At 7.0 miles the trail forks with the sign indicating access to Tenderfoot Pass, Hawkins Pass, and the return to Indian Crossing.

RECREATION: Below the Blue Hole, Rainbow Trout are the dominant species of fish. Above the Blue Hole, Dolly Varden are most common.

This trail provides access to a vast area of good hunting, but pack animals are often a necessity. The large trees and rock formations in the middle of this sector of trail are visual attractions — as is the Imnaha River.

The lower and upper parts of this section of the trail have many good camping sites.

COMMENTS: This trail is one main route of access into the heart of the Eagle Cap Wilderness. Trail use is light in the spring and gradually increases throughout the summer months — culminating in heavy usage during the hunting seasons. The area high above the trail on either side is excellent hunting or viewing habitat for "bench-legged" mule deer.

Several loop hikes can be taken from Trail No. 1816 varying in length from overnight to several days. One of the best is from Indian Crossing up the North Fork of the Imnaha to Tenderfoot Pass, then over Polaris Pass to the West Fork of the Wallowa River, then through the Lake Basin by one of several routes to Hawkins Pass, and back down the South Fork of the Imnaha to Indian Crossing. The possibilities are endless.

10 McCULLY

FOREST SERVICE TRAIL NO. 1812

SEASONAL ACCESS: June through November. The lower reaches can be hiked earlier in the year. Cross-country skiers use the trail into McCully Basin from December through April.

ELEVATION: 6,000' to 7,800' from the trailhead to McCully Basin. The pass between McCully and Sheep Creek drainages is 8,800'.

DIRECTIONS TO TRAILHEAD: Drive east 5.4 miles from Joseph on the Imnaha Highway 350. Turn right on Tucker Down Road. The road is gravel and it is clearly signed. You'll pass a handsome octagonal barn as you drive south. (In general, the mountains are to the south when you are hiking or driving in Wallowa County. This is a source of disorientation for some people.) At 3.3 miles you will pass a cattle guard. Stay on this main gravel road for another 1.5 miles. Immediately after crossing McCully Creek, the trailhead is located on the right.

TRAILHEAD SPECIFICS: The trailhead (A) is obvious and is marked with a USFS sign identifying the trail as McCully. There is a small but usually adequate parking lot.
  The nearest water is in McCully Creek. This water should be boiled before drinking due to the possibility of contamination by upstream hikers and wild and domestic animals. There is a stock unloading ramp and hitching rail at the trailhead.

TRAIL DISTANCE: The distance from the trailhead to McCully Basin (B) is approximately 6.25 miles. The distance on the trail from the basin on up to the pass is about 1.5 miles.

TRAIL CHARACTER: The trail is generally a moderate uphill climb with a couple steep but short pitches in the "4-5 mile" area. It is in very good condition, is quite wide in places, and is obvious all the way up to McCully Basin. The lush vegetation in the basin obscures the trail in places but it is easy to pick up again by looking around. The elevation gain from the trailhead to the basin is about 1,850 feet. Perennial creeks cross the trail at 1.25 miles, 4 miles, and at 5.25 miles; in early summer there are more creek cross ings. Early in the hiking season these creeks present minor obstacles to hikers (no bridges), but all are fairly easy to cross by rock-hopping. The trail parallels McCully Creek all the way to the basin, never being more than a few hundred yards away.

LANDMARKS AND POINTS OF INTEREST: In the first mile, the trail crosses McCully Creek and follows an old logging and fire road up the west side of the creek. The next 2-3 miles of trail follow through clearings burned in 1989 interspersed with thickets of Lodgepole Pine and Engelmann Spruce. The understory is profuse Grouse Huckleberry, which ripen in August and are a treat for hikers as well as local wildlife. Only one small creek crosses the trail in the first 2.5 miles, but you are never out of earshot of McCully Creek (named for F.D. McCully who is remembered as the "Father of Wallowa County"). This creek provides irrigation water to many farms downstream in the upper Prairie Creek section of Wallowa Valley. At 3.25 miles the trail crosses into the Eagle Cap Wilderness. Here you enter a stand of timber that has never been logged. The trees are obviously larger and older than the ones you have just come through. The Engelmann Spruce are slowly giving way to Subalpine Fir. At 4 miles you cross a creek that shows unmistakable signs of high springtime water flow. From mid-summer on, the crossing is easily made by rock-hopping. The final 2 miles to the basin begin to open up a little, offering tempting views of the ridges and peaks surrounding McCully Creek. At about 5.25 miles you cross a fork of McCully Creek and reach the lower end of the basin. Continue up the trail or cross-country explore in the area.

RECREATION: Campsites are limited before you reach the basin due to thick brush and trees and steep slopes. The basin is at least one-half mile long and one-fourth mile wide with many flat open meadows, pockets of trees, and brooks that provide numerous excellent campsites. The lower 3-4 miles of trail pass through second-growth Lodgepole/Spruce forest that provides good habitat for spruce grouse, gray jays, and goshawks and other accipiters. Lots of huckleberries grow along the first 4 miles of trail. Deer, elk, and black bear live in this area, as do numerous smaller mammals. Cross-country hiking in and around the basin provides spectacular views and photographic possibilities. Lots of wildflowers decorate the trailside, especially in the meadows of the basin. The trail is also used in winter for camping and cross-country ski-touring. The road to the trailhead is usually plowed and open during the winter.

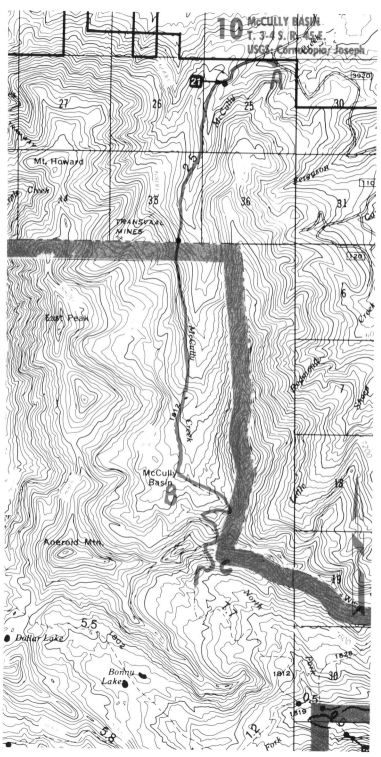

COMMENTS: Although the basin can be a destination in itself, it is also the gateway to further explorations. In addition to walking through the flower-studded meadows (keep an eye out for the striking and aptly-named Elephanthead), you can circle the basin on ridgetops. Don't forget to scan the slopes for bighorn sheep. Continuing south on the trail will lead you to the top of the divide (C) between McCully and Sheep Creek drainages and then down to Sheep Creek itself. From here, trails can take you east to Salt Creek Summit (and the Joseph-Halfway loop road), or westward over Tenderfoot Pass to the Wallowa River drainage or to Aneroid Lake.

11 MT. HOWARD GONDOLA—ANEROID LAKE

This hike is different in that it utilizes the Mt. Howard Gondola to gain the first 3,500' in elevation. The first actual hiking then goes cross-country, bushwhacking and rough terrain, to Aneroid Lake. These aspects make an interesting option to hiking up and back on the Aneroid Lake Trail.

FOREST SERVICE TRAIL NO. 1804 — Aneroid Lake

ELEVATION: 4,500'—9,500'

SEASONAL ACCESS: June—September

DIRECTIONS TO TRAILHEAD: From Joseph, stay on Main Street through town (Hwy. 82) and continue 6 miles to the head of Wallowa Lake. The highway branches at the head of the lake—take the left fork marked "Mt. Howard Gondola." Go about 0.25 miles and the base station for the gondola is on the left and well signed. If you continue another 0.75 miles up the highway to the end of the pavement, you reach the trailhead for Aneroid Lake Trail No. 1804. This is where the hike ends.

TRAILHEAD SPECIFICS: The base of the Gondola (A) is located in the recreation area around Wallowa Lake State Park. There is plenty of camping available although reservations may be needed during the summer. There is plenty of parking available at the gondola; there are also restrooms, picnic tables, and several nearby cafes.

TRAIL DISTANCE: It is a rugged 5 miles from the top of the gondola (B) on Mt. Howard along the ridge south to Aneroid Lake (C). If one decides to hike along the ridge and climb Aneroid Mt. (the third highest point in the Wallowas at 9,702') before descending to Aneroid Lake, the distance would be about 6 miles. From Aneroid Lake to the trailhead (D) and highway on Trail No. 1804 is 6.0 miles.

TRAIL CHARACTER: Although there is no trail for the first part of this hike, the terrain is comparable to many trails. Following the ridgetop south from the top of the gondola, one soon comes in view of Aneroid Lake. The ridgetop is open and one can usually stay to the east side of any peaks and maintain a level route. It's more fun to climb a bit and top three peaks over 9,000' including Aneroid Mt. and East

Peak. Glissading on snow fields under Aneroid Mt. is possible throughout most of the summer. There are some swampy areas between the ridgetop and Aneroid Lake, so pick a dry ridge for a descent. The more southerly dotted line on our map is a bit longer descent, but it is also more gentle and drier.

Trail No. 1804 is easily picked up between Roger Lake and Aneroid Lake. It is well-maintained down to the trailhead. There are no bad stream crossings and water is available. The trail drops about 3,000' in 6 miles and there are switchbacks galore. Take it easy downhill and save your knees.

LANDMARKS AND POINTS OF INTEREST: The view hiking along the ridge south from the gondola is spectacular. You look down into glacially-carved valleys and cirques on either side, and you can see the moraines on either side of Wallowa Lake—some of the most perfect in existence. Looking west into the Eagle Caps, you see formations of granite, basalt, greenstone and limestone. It's a geological wonderland. Looking east, you gaze across Hells Canyon and see the Seven Devils Range in Idaho.

Water pipits, rosy finches, and kestrel nest along the ridgetop. Mule deer and bighorn sheep frequent the open meadows, and golden-mantled squirrels will eat out of your hand. The Eagle Cap Wilderness boundary is about one mile south of the gondola.

Descending from the ridgetop you hike through clusters of wild flowers—monkey flower, gentian, and elephant-head are some of the showiest. The small lake east of Aneroid Lake is Roger Lake. The trail is just west of Roger Lake.

There are many good campsites around Aneroid and Roger Lake. Be sure to check wilderness regulations for camping distances from the lakes. There are also several cabins owned by a private concern at the head of Aneroid Lake.

Descending on Trail No. 1804, the first 2 miles are a gradual decline through open meadows flanked by lodgepole pine, alpine fir, and willow clumps where Lincoln sparrows nest. The last 4 miles drop steeply out of the basin through spruce and fir thickets. About 1.5 miles from the trailhead, the trail passes an old reservoir in the East Fork Wallowa River used for storing water piped down to the hydroelectric plant at the trailhead. The plant is still in use.

RECREATION: Bring your camera, your field guides to birds and wildflowers, and your binoculars. Fishing is excellent

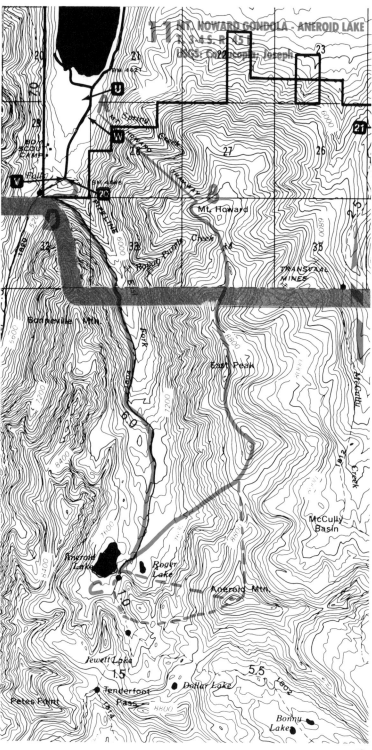

in the summer months for brook trout in both Roger and Aneroid lakes. Mosquitoes can be thick around Roger and Aneroid lakes in June and July—bring insect repellent. Aneroid Lake has fairly heavy use from campers in July and August. The area is not heavily used during hunting season in proportion to other areas in the county.

COMMENTS: One should be in very good condition and an experienced hiker to enjoy the hike and the altitude. This is not a USFS recognized trail, nor is it maintained; however, one person did leave the base of the gondola at 2:00 PM, rode up and hiked to Roger Lake by 4:30 PM, caught a limit of brook trout fly-fishing, and was back to his car by 8:30 PM. It is a great hike with just a day pack.

Some people prefer hiking uphill—it's easier on the knees. The hike can be taken in reverse—just be sure to purchase a gondola ticket at the base so you will have one to ride down when you reach the top.

Unnamed ridge just south of Aneroid Mtn. Photo from trail to Aneroid Lake. (Justin Bohannon photo)

12 WEST FORK WALLOWA RIVER — LAKES BASIN

FOREST SERVICE TRAIL NOS. 1820, 1810 - 1810A, 1806

ELEVATION: 4,800' — 8,400'

SEASONAL ACCESS: Trail open to Six Mile Meadow by mid-June — to the high lakes from early July until mid-October.

DIRECTIONS TO TRAILHEAD: Proceed south from Joseph on State Highway 82 following the signs to Wallowa Lake. When you reach the south end of the lake, about 6 miles from Joseph, you will come to a junction in the paved road. Turn left and follow Powerhouse Road to the parking lot at the end of the pavement — approximately one mile. The trailhead (A) is located up the hill and to the left of the powerhouse. It can be found by following the closed road behind the trailhead sign about 200 feet up the hill to the bulletin board marking the beginning of the trail.

TRAILHEAD SPECIFICS: The Wallowa Lake Trailhead is equipped with a trailhead sign, bulletin board with trail map, destination and mileage signs, hitch racks, and a horse loading ramp. There is plenty of parking for cars and trucks. Restrooms, water, and picnic facilities are available during the summer months at South Wallowa Lake State Park, directly across the road to the west of the trailhead. There are no camping facilities at the trailhead. The nearest camping facilities are at Wallowa Lake State Park (reservations required during summer months). Maps of the wilderness and mountain weather information are available at the USFS Visitor Center 300 yards down the road.

TRAIL DISTANCE: Six Mile Meadow makes a nice 12 mile round trip for a day hike. One way trail distance to Frazier Lake is 10.0 miles; 12.0 miles to Glacier Lake. An overnight or weekend trip into the Lakes Basin via the West Fork Wallowa River would be approximately 25 - 30 miles. A 27-mile loop trip can be made by going up the West Fork, through the Lakes Basin, over Glacier Pass to Glacier and Frazier Lakes (Trail No. 1806), returning via the West Fork Wallowa River.

TRAIL CHARACTER: The West Fork Wallowa River and Lakes Basin trails are well maintained and provide easy travel for hikers and horsemen, and are well suited for family groups. Because this trail is so readily accessible it receives heavy use by horses and hikers alike. The heavy horse traffic can create some dust, horse manure, and attract abundant flies in the first 3 miles at the height of the summer season.

The West Fork Wallowa River Trail No. 1820 is a well-graded trail. From the trailhead at 4,900' the trail gains 1,100' to Six Mile Meadow. From there the trail gains another 1,200' in the next 4 miles to Frazier Lake, and 800' in the 2 miles to Glacier Lake. From Six Mile Meadow the Lakes Basin Trail No. 1810 climbs 1,200' to Horseshoe Lake in 3 miles. The hike over to Glacier Lake via Glacier Pass is a fairly steep climb to 8,400' at the pass.

All of the major trail junctions are signed in the Eagle Cap Wilderness.

There are only minor stream crossings along the West Fork Trail and up to the Lakes Basin. If you continue up to Frazier Lake on the West Fork Trail you will have to ford the West Fork Wallowa River at 9 miles. There is a log across the river approximately 200 yards downstream from the ford that can be crossed with caution. There is water readily available along this trail throughout the season; however, you will want to carry water on the 3-mile section of trail that climbs up to the Lakes Basin.

LANDMARKS AND POINTS OF INTEREST: The West Fork Wallowa River Trail follows the river to its headwater at Glacier Lake. The trail starts out in a mixed conifer forest dominated by Grand Fir, Douglas Fir, Western Larch, and Ponderosa Pine. The first mile of trail is fairly steep, taking a series of quick switchbacks to the National Forest and Eagle Cap Wilderness boundaries within the first half mile. At the top of the hill by the wilderness boundary take a breather and look back for a nice view of Wallowa Lake and the east moraine. After this initial climb, the trail flattens out and follows closely along the river.

Keep your eyes open for indications of past land slides and avalanches. At 1.5 miles the trail passes through an extensive blowdown caused by an avalanche that occurred during the winter of 1986. If you look up the valley wall, you will be able to see where winds generated by the avalanche snapped off all of the trees in its path as it came down the mountain. The trail continues to follow the river, passing through dense forests interspersed with openings created by past avalanches. This is a great place to look for wildflowers in the early summer. Mountain Bluebells, Forget-me-nots, Paintbrush, Columbine, and Cow Parsnip

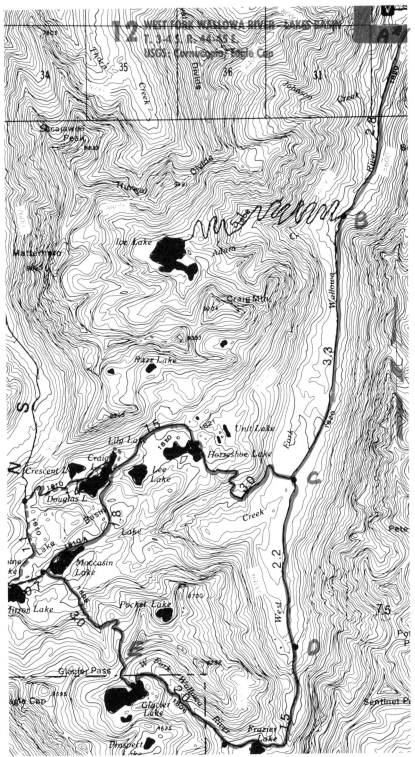

are abundant in the meadows; Lady Slippers, Calypso Orchids, and Coral Root are found in the forest communities.

At 2.8 miles you will come to the junction (B) to the Ice Lake Trail No. 1808. The West Fork Wallowa River Trail continues to the left. At 3.0 miles there is a good view of the confluence of the West Fork Wallowa and Adams Creek — the outlet stream from Ice Lake. The trail continues on through the forest and occasional small meadows to Six Mile Meadow, a relatively large meadow. This is a nice place for a lunch stop for fishing in the river. This is also one of the first places you can get a view of the surrounding mountains. If you have planned to only go this far, it is well worth the time to hike another mile up the trail toward the Lakes Basin. The trail begins climbing up out of the valley and at about 7.0 miles there is an excellent spot to view the Martin Bridge limestone formations of the upper West Fork drainage and the west face of Pete's Point with its interesting folded and metamorphosed formations. Six Mile Meadow has been closed to overnight camping and grazing of horses to allow the vegetation to recover. Good camping spots can be found in the surrounding forest or further up the West Fork Trail.

The junction (C) of the West Fork Wallowa Trail and the Lakes Basin Trail lies at the beginning of the meadow. If you are continuing on to the High Lakes, you have a choice to make at Six Mile Meadow. The trail to the right climbs up to Horseshoe Lake and other lakes in the Lakes Basin. To the left the trail follows the river up to its headwaters in Frazier and Glacier Lakes.

The West Fork Trail continues south from Six Mile Meadow up the valley toward Frazier Lake — passing through meadows and forest. At 8.0 miles the trail climbs through a large avalanche meadow to the junction (D) of the Polaris Pass Trail. This is another good place to view an abundance of wildflowers. The junction to Polaris Pass is near the top of the meadow. The trail to the left leads over Polaris Pass, and the right-hand trail continues up to Frazier Lake. After the junction the trail re-enters the forest and skirts the edge of a narrow gorge before entering a series of subalpine meadows. You will probably feel like you have finally entered the high country in this valley. You are surrounded by impressive limestone cliffs and waterfalls, and wildflowers are abundant. Keep your eyes open for bighorn sheep and mountain goats that have occasionally been seen on the surrounding cliffs. Approximately 9.0 miles up the trail you will have to ford the West Fork Wallowa River. Late in the summer the ford is easy to do in tennis shoes; however, the crossing can be treacherous in July and early August. An alternative to getting your feet wet is crossing a log that spans the river approximately 250 yards down river from the ford. Once you have crossed the river, it is another mile up a rocky, steep trail to Frazier Lake.

Beyond Frazier Lake, it is another 2 spectacular miles to Glacier Lake. The trail, newly constructed in 1986, follows the north side of the valley and has splendid views of the

Moccasin Lake. (Stanlynn Daugherty photo)

surrounding countryside. From Glacier Lake it is a short, intense climb to the top of Glacier Pass (E) at 8,400', and another 2.5 miles from the pass to the Lakes Basin. From Glacier Lake it is a gradual 1,000' climb west across the remains of Benson Glacier to the summit of Eagle Cap. This probably affords the best view of the entire wilderness area. The Benson Glacier was the last remaining glacier in the Wallowa Mtns.

The Lakes Basin encompasses eight named lakes including Mirror, Moccasin, Upper Sunshine, Lee, Crescent, Douglas, and Horseshoe. There is a 5-mile loop trail in the Basin that takes you by the majority of these lakes. This area is very scenic but can get crowded in the summer months. From the Lakes Basin you can make a loop trip back down to Six Mile Meadow via Trail No. 1810.

Deer are commonly seen in these drainages and elk are occasionally seen in the Frazier Lake vicinity. Bears can be a problem at Six Mile Meadow and in the Lakes Basin. You will need to hang your food. Also commonly seen are squirrels and chipmunks, and pika are common in the boulder fields. Birds you may see include Mountain Chickadee, Clark's Nutcracker, Gray Jay, woodpeckers, and an occasional Goshawk if you're lucky. There are no poisonous snakes in the Eagle Cap but there are mosquitoes in the summer months in the Lakes Basin — carry insect repellent.

RECREATION: Fishing is good in most lakes and the West Fork Wallowa for Brook and Rainbow trout. Camping sites abound. Photo opportunities are unlimited. If you're a member of a polar bear club, you will enjoy swimming in the Lakes Basin. The trails are used by a few people for cross-country skiing; however, this is serious avalanche territory. Take extreme safety precautions.

COMMENTS: Remember to observe Forest Service regulations while camping or hiking in the wilderness. Camping is prohibited within 200 feet of the lakes to protect the lakeshore vegetation. An active program to restore native vegetation to "beat-out" lakeshores has been carried on since 1980 by Forest Service volunteers. Many people think that Mirror Lake is the prettiest in the Lakes Basin. See it by all means, but we advise that you not plan to camp near Mirror. It does get a lot of use and this is fragile country. So others may enjoy the trail after you have traveled through, please pack out all of your trash and cigarette butts, and — leave the flowers for others to study and enjoy.

13 CHIEF JOSEPH

FOREST SERVICE TRAIL NO. 1803

ELEVATION: 4,700' — 7,600'

DIRECTIONS TO TRAILHEAD: See Hike #12. Follow Highway 82 south from Joseph along Wallowa Lake, past the gondola to the end of the pavement and the trailhead.

TRAILHEAD SPECIFICS: See Hike #12. Plenty of parking, camping and picnicking, stock ramps, water, toilets, etc.

TRAIL DISTANCE: From the trailhead (A) to the end of the trail (B) is about 7.5 miles. The roundtrip hike would be 15.0 miles. However, this is an excellent trail to hike as far as you want and then return to the trailhead.

TRAIL CHARACTER: The trail is well maintained and easy to follow for its entire length. The first 0.3 miles on Trail No. 1820 is the steepest grade on the entire trail. The remainder of the hike on Trail No. 1803 (about 7.2 miles) is a steady climb, after you cross the West Fork Wallowa River, of about 3,000' in 7 miles. It is a gentle walking grade. There are two major streams to cross on the trail — West Fork Wallowa River and BC Creek. Both have

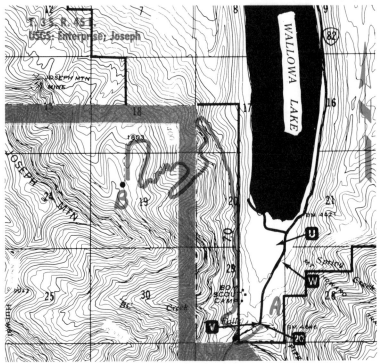

excellent bridges. After crossing BC Creek, there is one more very small stream at about the 3.5 mile mark. This is the last water on the trail. Be sure to carry water if you are going past this point.

LANDMARKS AND POINTS OF INTEREST: The first 0.3 miles is on the West Fork Wallowa Trail No. 1820. At the junction of Trail No. 1803 turn right. There is a sign denoting Chief Joseph Trail. The trail goes down to the Wallowa River where a beautiful bridge crosses the swift flowing stream — then switchbacks up the east bank where it heads north again to parallel the campground and Wallowa Lake below. The next 2.5 miles is a gentle hike under majestic cliffs, across boulder fields, and through tall forests of pine and fir. Along this section of the trail, watch for dippers when you cross the Wallowa River and note the Mountain Mahogany growing on the open slopes along the switchbacks above the bridge. The trees with small, velvety leaves are a favorite deer and elk browse and remind one of small acacia trees on the African plain. Also along this section look for pikas in the rock fields and for hummingbirds, fly-catchers, and warblers along the edges of openings.

At about the 3.5 mile mark the trail switches back to the south, enters the Eagle Cap Wilderness Area, and then climbs gradually to open meadows of grass and sage. The final portion of the trail switches up through thickets of Lodgepole Pine and Alpine Fir interspersed with open meadows. Blue Grouse and Mule Deer frequent these areas. The trail ends in high meadows overlooking the Wallowa Valley, and behind the meadows — the sheer faces of Chief Joseph Mountain loom up.

RECREATION: This is primarily a hike to view flora, fauna, geological formations, and great scenery in all directions. Fishing and hunting are minimal — in fact, the first 1.5 miles of the hike is in an area where hunting is prohibited. The only good campsites occur at the end of the trail — and they are dry camps. However, where the trail crosses the Wallowa River at about 0.75 miles and where it crosses BC Creek at about 1.5 are two of the most scenic spots on any hike in Wallowa County.

COMMENTS: For visitors to Wallowa Lake State Park a nice circle hike is up to the trailhead, onto the trail for about 2.2 miles until above the park, and then down the hill to the park — only several hundred yards below. Be careful on this last leg to the park. There are non-maintained trails, but they are quite steep. If you take your time there will be no problems.

14   ECHO LAKE

FOREST SERVICE TRAIL NOS. 1807, 1824

SEASONAL ACCESS: Summer and fall.

ELEVATION: 5,000′ at the trailhead to 8,400′ at Echo Lake.

DIRECTIONS TO TRAILHEAD: Hurricane Creek Trailhead (A) is located 10 miles due south of Enterprise and 7 miles southwest of Joseph. It is reached by taking the Hurricane Creek Road from Enterprise south to the corner at the Hurricane Creek Grange hall, then proceeding straight ahead on the gravel road 5 miles to the parking area. The road is well signed.

From Joseph turn west at the Chevron station and go 2 miles on the paved road to the same Grange hall and turn left.

Please note that this area is subject to flash flooding and at times the road or trail may be blocked at a relatively low elevation. Local inquiry at the USFS office is advised when planning your trip.

Echo Lake. (Stanlynn Daugherty photo)

TRAILHEAD SPECIFICS: A primitive campground is located halfway up the secondary road with 6 or 8 sites having fire rings and tables. A stock unloading ramp, hitching rails, and a pit toilet are located at the trailhead parking area.

TRAIL DISTANCE: The distance from the trailhead to Echo Lake is 8.5 miles.

TRAIL CHARACTER: Although the first 5.5 miles of trail are relatively easy hiking, the area is subject to avalanche debris blocking the trail as late as July — especially 3 miles from the trailhead at Slick Rock Creek. Water is available at regular intervals and the only major stream crossing is at Falls Creek in the first .25 mile of trail. Snow can cover the trail in protected areas until early July.

The trail from Hurricane Creek up to Echo Lake is not maintained for packstock. It is steep and rocky as it climbs out of the valley, rising 2,400' in just over 2 miles.

LANDMARKS AND POINTS OF INTEREST: Crossing Falls Creek shortly after leaving the parking area, the trail follows Hurricane Creek for the first 5.5 miles. After climbing the first short rise, the traveler is rewarded with a stunning view of Sacajawea Peak — at 9,833' it is the second highest in the Eagle Cap Wilderness. At the wilderness boundary, at the 1-mile mark, is a section of fallen logs that are the result of winds accompanying a massive avalanche in the spring of 1986.

Flower-filled meadows alternate with shady woods as the trail gently climbs for 2.5 miles before it switches back up to a narrow gorge where Hurricane Creek cuts through the marbled side of Sacajawea near Slick Rock Creek. From this point it is a short 3 miles to the Echo Lake Trail junction (B). It is signed and is located just before the main Trail No. 1807 crosses Hurricane Creek. Turning right and crossing a small bog, Trail No. 1824 begins its steep rise toward Echo Lake through larch and fir stands. A small stream is crossed after the first mile. Fill water containers here since the next 1.5 mile is steep, dry, and open; however, one now has fine views of the valley below and adjacent peaks including the highest in the Wallowas — the Matterhorn at 9,845.'

The trail continues its unrelenting ascent to a small meadow. Travelers with stock may wish to camp on its edge as feed is vary sparse at the lake. The last 0.5 mile climbs through granite outcroppings to finally reach this lovely alpine lake nestled below serrated ridges. Located at 8,400,' the lake can still be partially ice-covered well into July.

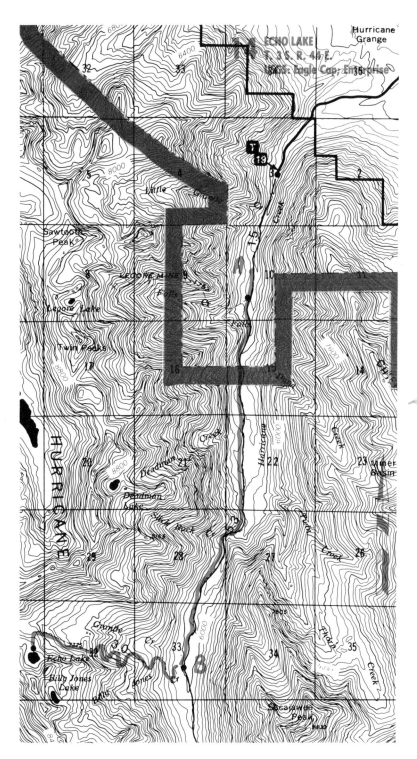

ECHO LAKE
T. 3 S. R. 44 E.
USGS: Eagle Cap, Enterprise

Hurricane
Grange

RECREATION: Campsites are all along the trail following Hurricane Creek. At Echo Lake there are campsites available but no wood, so bring a small camp stove. The lake contains small, tasty Brook Trout. Fishing is also good in Billy Jones Lake which is located about 0.5 miles south over a boulder-covered ridge.

A short hike up the west ridge above Echo Lake offers splendid views of the Lostine River Canyon. It is possible to see Mule Deer, elk, bighorn sheep and mountain goats in this area.

In August the Grouse Whortleberries are ripening and a variety of wildflowers are present throughout the summer and early fall. Be sure to pack lots of film, a fishing rod and binoculars to enjoy this challenging but rewarding journey.

COMMENTS: Plenty of time should be allowed for this hike, especially the last 3 miles; and especially if you are carrying a full pack. It may be best to camp close to the junction of the Hurricane Creek and Echo Lake trails and continue the remainder of the hike into Echo Lake the second day. For the in-shape hiker, it is possible to carry a smaller pack and go up to Echo Lake on a day hike.

Llama packing on Hurricane Creek. (Stanlynn Daugherty photo)

15 FRANCES LAKE

FOREST SERVICE TRAIL NO. 1663

SEASONAL ACCESS: May to November on the lower portions of the trail. There may be snow banks until July on the highest part of the trail. The road to the trailhead is closed during late fall and winter.

ELEVATION: 5,300' — 8,600'

DIRECTIONS TO TRAILHEAD: From Lostine on Highway 82, take the paved county road south. This road is an extension of Main Street in Lostine. Stay on this road 15.7 miles to the trailhead. The first 7.1 miles to the USFS boundary is paved. From the boundary it is 5.0 miles to Lake Creek Guard Station on bumpy, gravel road, and then another 3.6 miles to the trailhead. The final portion of the road can be rough and dusty during certain times of the year.

TRAIL SPECIFICS: At the trailhead (A) there is a sign on the left side of the road denoting Frances Lake Trail No. 1663.

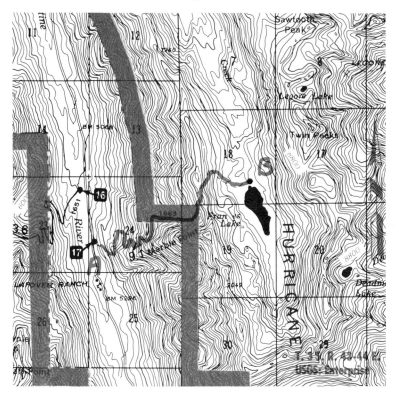

There is limited parking at the trailhead, but nearby Lillyville campground has ample parking, water, pit toilets, and a stock unloading ramp. There is much less chance of having your vehicle dented if you park at the campground.

TRAIL DISTANCE: From the trailhead (A) to Frances Lake (B) is a distance of 9 miles.

TRAIL CHARACTER: The Frances Lake Trail No. 1663 has an easy grade with numerous traverses and switchbacks. As one climbs higher the trail narrows — and passing or meeting other pack stock may present a problem. If you are using horses it would be wise to send a person ahead to find a trail turnout in case another party is encountered on the trail. The trail does not present any difficulties for hikers. Early in the season (until July usually) there may be snow and ice along the north side of the base of Marble Point, which is located about two-thirds of the way to the ridge top. Because of the many switchbacks one will travel several times the direct vertical distance.

LANDMARKS AND POINTS OF INTEREST: The lower portion of the trail is a series of switchbacks which gradually lift you out of the valley floor through different species of timber. Be sure to carry some water since little is available on the trail. The hike is initially remarkable for views across the Lostine canyon, various species of trees including Lodgepole Pine and Douglas Fir, and a variety of scenery.

Flowering plants are abundant in the lower elevations during the summer months; these include several varieties of penstemon, paintbrush, and Sego Lily. Huckleberries can be found along the trail later in July.

During July one can photograph the unique alpine flora along the higher sections of the trail. Alpine forget-me-nots, several species of dryads, and many buckwheats bloom abundantly during the short summer season. Also at this elevation one finds stands of dead White Pine where mountain bluebirds and dark-eyed juncos nest during the summer months. Above timberline in some of the rocky drainages you will perhaps see some of the rarer alpine species of birds that nest here such as the (gray-crowned) Rosy Finch and Water Pipit.

RECREATION: In the vicinity of the north base of Marble Point there is an open basin with protected campsites in its lower portion. The trail then passes over a high ridge and descends into Frances Lake basin. The best camping sites here are south of the lake at the edge of the timber where a breeze will assist in keeping away any insect pests.

Fishing is usually very good and hunting can be good in the basin. Deer, elk, bighorn sheep, and mountain goats can be seen in the area if one is observant. The upper drainage into the lake is unique for alpine flora species and for birds that inhabit the terrain in summer. For people who like to explore there are ponds and small lakes below Frances Lake that contain fish. Further down one will find excellent stream fishing for Brook Trout and a few Rainbow, extensive meadows, and interesting water pours or falls. An old trail leads one down the sunny side of Lake Creek. This old pack trail is not maintained at the present time.

COMMENTS: The prime season for use in the area is July to October. The geology of the area is fascinating. One encounters extensive limestone-marble formations, granite, and sedimentary series. East of the lake and high on the ridge the terrain is of volcanic origin. Plan to camp in this area long enough to explore the alpine country. The area is never heavily used and you may often be the only party camped at the lake.

Frances Lake Trail near base of Marble Point. (Bill George photo)

16 BOWMAN TRAIL — CHIMNEY LAKE
JOHN HENRY LAKE

FOREST SERVICE TRAIL NO. 1651

SEASONAL ACCESS: The road up the Lostine River to the trailhead may not be open until June. The trail may not have all the snowbanks melted out until mid-July. The road and trail usually remain open until November.

ELEVATION: 5,200' — 8,200'

DIRECTIONS TO TRAILHEAD: See the directions to trailhead on Hike #15 — Frances Lake. The Bowman Trail trailhead is 15.1 miles from the Highway 82 turnoff in Lostine. The trailhead is on the right side of the road and 0.6 miles before you reach the Frances Lake Trailhead.

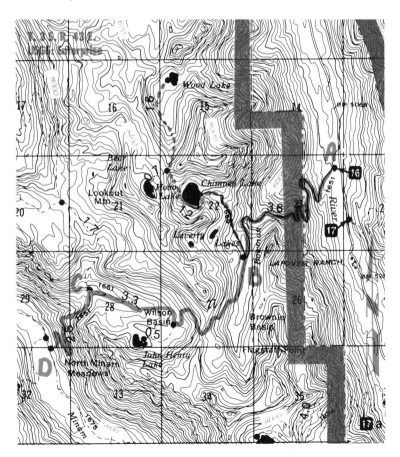

TRAILHEAD SPECIFICS: The sign at the trailhead reads: Bowman Trail No. 1651; Chimney Lake 5; John Henry Lake 6; North Minam Meadows 10.

A stock loading ramp is located 100 yards south of the trailhead. There are parking spaces at both the trailhead and the loading ramp. The concrete trail bridge across the Lostine River is the beginning of the trail. There are no immediate campsites at the trailhead, but many are close-by up and down the Lostine River.

TRAIL DISTANCE: From the trailhead (A) to the junction of Trail No. 1659 (B) in Brownie Basin is 3.6 miles. From this junction it is about 1.0 mile to Laverty Lakes, 1.5 miles to Chimney Lake, and about 3.0 miles to Wood Lake. Hobo Lake is about 2.0 from the junction. All these lakes lie on or close to Trail No. 1659. If you stay on Trail 1659 it is 5.0 miles from the trailhead to John Henry Lake. It is 7.0 miles on Trail No. 1651 from the trailhead to the junction of Trail No. 1653 (C) which follows down Bear Creek. The Bowman Trail concludes at North Minam Meadows (D) which is a short 10.0 miles from the trailhead.

TRAIL CHARACTER: The trail is in good shape, but switchbacks many times to Brownie Basin. The hiker should consciously hold back (to a restrained pace) for the first hour and a half. One could make very good time initially and then suffer deep tiredness.

Water is available in several places but not continuously. Stream crossings are minor later in the season, but can be particularly dangerous early when the June snowpack is melting.

The trailhead is about 5,200' in elevation with a climb to 7,300' in Brownie Basin, another 200' rise to Laverty Lake, and then on to 7,600' at Chimney Lake. The saddle beyond is another 500' in elevation followed by a drop to 7,400' at Wood Lake.

The hike up through Brownie Basin on Trail No. 1651 climbs across open meadows full of wildflowers to a saddle 7,800' in elevation. The trail then drops through scattered patches of Alpine Fir and White Pine on its way to Wilson Basin and John Henry Lake. The final part of the trail drops down to North Minam Meadows with a series of switchbacks. There is little water on this portion of the trail. The trail is well maintained and the views are spectacular.

LANDMARKS AND POINTS OF INTEREST: At about 3 miles from the trailhead, the trail crosses the stream from

Brownie Basin. In another 20 mimutes the hiker reaches the basin — a good spot to camp. One-half mile past the lower end of the basin, the trail forks. The trail sign indicates Chimney Lake, Wilson Basin, and Lostine Canyon. Trail No. 1659 to Chimney Lake is the object of this following description.

About 1 mile from the junction, the trail passes the lower of the Laverty Lakes. At the break of morning light, this area is good for observing the seeming flourescence of lichens on the rocks. Chimney Lake is only a few minutes hike past Laverty Lakes. The trail then goes through talus slopes, which are excellent viewing areas for pika, to a saddle. At the top, a side hike to Hobo Lake can be started. The descent to Wood Lake should be slow to protect knees and ankles. The delicate foliage of conifers is Mountain Hemlock.

From the previous trail junction it is about 1.5 miles on Trail No. 1651 to the pass between Brownie Basin and Wilson Basin. From this point there are great views east to the Lostine Canyon and west to John Henry Lake and the Minam River drainage. The side trail to John Henry Lake takes off to the left about one-half mile down the trail from the pass.

RECREATION: There is fishing for Eastern Brook Trout in Brownie Basin, North Minam Meadows, and all the lakes. Wood and Hobo lakes were once planted with Golden Trout but have since reverted back to populations of Eastern Brook Trout.

Hunting is good in the area, but since it is so vast, one may want to consider using pack animals.

On the initial part of Trail No. 1659 to Laverty Lakes there are excellent views of Twin Peaks to the east and of Eagle Cap to the south past Flagstaff Point.

Most people would consider the middle of October as the end of the hiking season in the area. However, late September and early October hikes in this area have a particular charm.

There are excellent campsites close to all the lakes and in the basins. Be sure to check the Forest Service regulations and camp away from lake shores in order to protect fragile vegetation. John Henry Lake, in particular, can have many mosquitoes early in the season.

This area affords a great opportunity for a circle hike which takes you to six different lakes. One can start at the trailhead and hike through Brownie Basin to John Henry Lake and then on to the junction with Trail No. 1653. Hike north on Trail No. 1653 for about 2 miles until you cross the outlet stream from Bear Lake. Follow up this stream to Bear Lake. From Bear Lake one can hike overland to Wood Lake — it is not a difficult route. A good topographical map would help on this last part of the hike. From Wood Lake one can take Trail No. 1659 back to Brownie Basin and then return to the trailhead.

COMMENTS: At one time Laverty Lakes were referred to on maps as Loverty Lakes. The original correct spelling has been restored. The corruption of Hebo to Hobo Lake has persisted. The dike formation in the mountain above Chimney Lake is the geological reason for that name. John Henry Lake and Wilson Basin (which includes John Henry Lake) were named after the prospector, John Henry Wilson. John Henry Wilson spent a winter at his diggings and found the winter not silent at all — but noisy with the sounds of snow slides and falling rocks.

Bridge across Lostine River at Bowman Trail. (Bob Jackson photo)

17   MAXWELL LAKE

FOREST SERVICE TRAIL NO. 1674

SEASONAL ACCESS: Summer and fall until the snow season.

ELEVATION: 5,520' — 7,760'

DIRECTIONS TO TRAILHEAD: The trailhead is located 17.5 miles south of Lostine on the Lostine River Road. It is located on the right side of the road (west side) and is marked with a Forest Service sign. See Hike #15 and #16.

TRAILHEAD SPECIFICS: Shady Campground is situated at the trailhead with a dozen primitive campsites including picnic tables, fire pits and toilets. The Lostine River is the only water source so bring or boil drinking water. There are no stock facilities located at the trailhead.

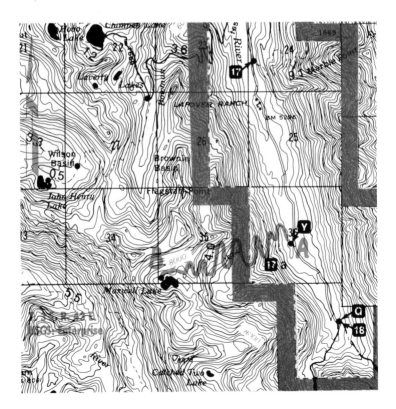

TRAIL DISTANCE: From the trailhead (A) to Maxwell Lake (B) is a distance of 4.0 miles.

TRAIL CHARACTER: The first 3 miles of the trail is a steady climb on well-graded switchbacks. Trailhead elevation is 5,520' and the lake is located at 7,760' for a net elevation gain of 2,240'. The last mile is not graded and climbs steeply up to the lake. There is a side-stream crossing located near the beginning of the trail which could be difficult during high water at the peak of the snow melt early in the year. Small side streams cross the trail along the first 3 miles but they can dry up later in the summer.

LANDMARKS AND POINTS OF INTEREST: The trail begins by crossing the Lostine River on a footbridge and shortly thereafter it crosses the outlet stream from Maxwell Lake. This rocky crossing may be difficult at high water.

The next 3 miles take the hiker steadily uphill, crossing steep avalanche meadows on a series of well-graded switchbacks. Small patches of larch/fir forest give shade and relief from the open meadows. Small side streams from snowmelt and springs cross the trail through the grandiorite boulders and from small riparian grottos. These streams may dwindle to a trickle later in the season so be sure to pack drinking water.

The view of the upper Lostine canyon near the East Fork and the West Fork junction is grand and halfway up the trail the dome of Eagle Cap may be seen in the distance.

The last mile of the trail climbs steeply on an occasionally deeply eroded trail to the lake. Located in a glacial cirque, Maxwell Lake is rimmed with granite walls. Fine groups of White Bark Pine grow on outcroppings along the lakeshore.

RECREATION: Small Eastern Brook Trout may be found in the lake and in a smaller un-named lake just to the southeast. Campsites are few, making this a good choice for a day hike. There is one site on the west end of the lake located near a small gravel beach. Grazing is minimal for stock so a good supply of supplemental feed should be carried.

COMMENTS: The trip to and from Maxwell Lake makes an excellent day hike. It is not too difficult a hike to climb the ridge behind Maxwell Lake. This affords one a view of North Minam Meadows and some of the lakes in the Minam drainage.

Another possibility for a day circle hike if one is ambitious is to climb to Maxwell Lake, then hike along the ridgeline south for about 1 mile to Catched Two Lake, then down to the West Fork of the Lostine (a tough hike with no trail to follow), wade the river (knee depth) and follow the trail on the west side down to the end of the road (about 1.0 mile). The trailhead to Maxwell Lake is another 1.5 miles down the road.

Maxwell Lake. (Forest Service photo)

18   LOSTINE — NORTH MINAM MEADOWS LOOP

This is a nine-day loop in the Eagle Cap Wilderness beginning at Bowman Trail No. 1651 trailhead and ending on East Fork Lostine River Trail No. 1662.

FOREST SERVICE TRAIL NO. Refer to map and text.

ELEVATION: 5,000' — 9,600'

DIRECTIONS TO TRAILHEAD: From Lostine, take the Lostine River Road, south, for 15.1 miles. The trailhead is on the right side of the road with a USFS trailhead sign denoting Bowman Trail. (same as Hike #16)

TRAILHEAD SPECIFICS: The sign at the trailhead gives distances to the lakes in the area and also to North Minam Meadows. There is a stock ramp about 100 yards south of the trailhead. There is adequate parking at the trailhead and at the stock ramp. There are many campsites along the Lostine River road, but none at the immediate site of the trailhead.

TRAIL DISTANCE: This loop covers about 80-90 miles without any overlapping. The distance covered each day varies from 5 to 13 miles depending on where one decides to camp.

TRAIL CHARACTER: The majority of trails described in this loop are well-marked and well-maintained. In the case of a cross-country section, such as around Eagle Lake or climbing Eagle Cap, one must use common sense as to the best route. The trails in the Eagle Cap Wilderness are usually passable by the middle of July although snow can linger in the passes until August. Storms can deposit new snow at any time of the year above 5,000.'

LANDMARKS AND POINTS OF INTEREST: This nine-day loop covers roughly 90 miles with numerous traverses, ascents, and descents virtually all in the Eagle Cap Wilderness.

The trip starts (A) at the Bowman Trailhead (see Hike #16) 15.1 miles up the Lostine River Canyon from Lostine. The Bowman Trail No. 1651 takes off across the Lostine River and heads up 3.6 miles of easy switchbacks into Brownie Basin. Keep to the left when two trails intersect in the basin and climb over an un-named pass into Wilson Basin. As the trail descends, look for a spur trail to your

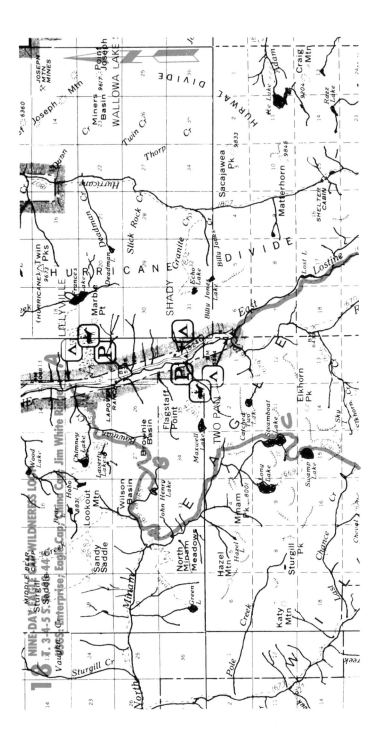

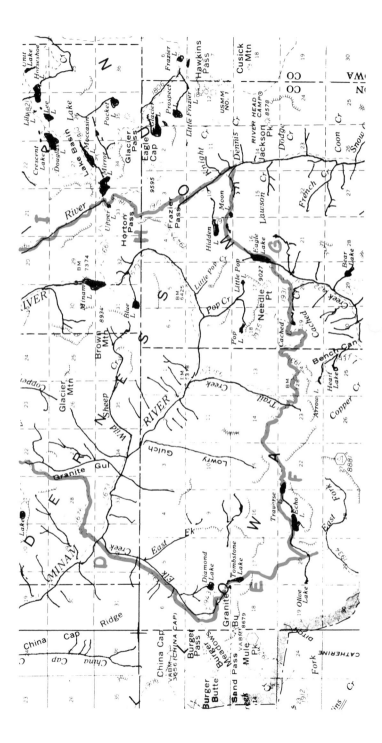

left which will lead 0.25 mile across an open meadow toward John Henry Lake. The trail is less noticeable while crossing the meadow, but once across you'll easily see the trail and lake. On the left side of the spur trail, look for an abandoned mine tunnel. It would be worth an investigation. (Beware that tunnels and caves are often sensitive habitat for bats, some species of which are considered endangered. They use energy they cannot afford to lose when they are unduly disturbed. Furthermore, although rabies or other infectious diseases are not epidemic, they are not unknown.) Total distance day one: 5.5 miles.

Trail No. 1651 descends 5.8 miles into North Minam Meadows (B) for the start of day two. Trail No. 1675 is at the bottom and is the one you'll be on for the next day or two. The trail is in good shape and ascends the North Fork of the Minam River gradually at first and then climbs up and into a large and impressive basin containing Steamboat Lake. Good campsites, fishing and relaxing scenery will be awaiting you at the lake. Total distance day two: 11.6 miles.

Trail No. 1675 continues around the southeastern corner of Steamboat Lake (C) and up a fairly steep ascent to Swamp Lake. The trail levels off for awhile before climbing up again onto a granite plateau, 3.2 miles from Steamboat Lake. Basalt caps and Glacier Mountain are on your left as you head across level terrain to a point overlooking the Minam River Valley. Here, Trail No. 1675 becomes No. 1676 which leads down 4.5 miles to the Minam River. This trail is in poor shape with windfall logs and rocky scree in various spots in the trail. Be careful hiking here. A drop of 3,000' over 4.5 miles into the valley makes for some burnt brake shoes at the bottom. There are very inspiring trees along the trail at midslope. Ponderosa Pine and Douglas Fir are huge and full of birds. Also along midslope, look for black bear. You may encounter a sow and cub for a brief moment. After all the dusty switchbacks, the Minam River becomes an oasis in the desert. There are numerous campsites just off the trail along the river. You will find Trail No. 1912 approximately 150 yards downstream from the junction of Trail No. 1676 and Trail No. 1673. Deer are everywhere and you may have to chase them off occasionally. Total distance day three: 8.2 miles.

Plan an easy ascent up Elk Creek (D) on Trail No. 1912 to Tombstone Lake. Traveling southwest into Union County, Tombstone Lake is just inside the Wilderness boundary guarded by solid Granite Butte. There is a nice lunch spot at the head of Elk Creek where Trail No. 1943 crosses and heads up to Tombstone Lake. The climb up to Tombstone

Lake is moderate and at several points you can see back across the Minam River Valley to the granite plateau above Granite Gulch drainage where you had been the day before. China Cap is now a prominent basalt cap to the northwest. At Tombstone Lake, biting gnats can be at their best!! Likewise — so can the fish! A "00" Mepps spinner keeps Rainbow Trout and Eastern Brook Trout busy for quite awhile. Total miles day four: 7.8 miles.

Next morning continue up Trail No. 1943 to a saddle between Tombstone Lake and West Eagle drainage (E). Moderate switchbacks into West Eagle offer many impressive views of the Echo Lake - Traverse Lake Basin. Stay on the trail and don't be tempted into traversing straight across into the basin. High brush and difficult sidehill travel make going down the trail and back up a lot easier. Once at the bottom of the West Eagle drainage, you'll ascend 2.6 miles of switchback up to Echo Lake. There you'll discover good campsites away from the lake and good swimming. Total distance day five: 8.2 miles.

Day six begins with a steady climb out of the basin to Wonker Pass (F), one of the highest passes in the Eagle Cap at 8,600.' There are superb views here to the northeast into the upper Minam River drainage and to the west toward Baker Valley. The trail descends 6.4 miles into the upper reaches of Trail Creek. Look for elk if you're moving through this area early in the morning. Trail No. 1931 heads up the left side of Trail Creek drainage to a pass at 8,500' before dropping down into Cached Lake. From the upper part of the trail you may see tremendous lightning storms brewing to the east or west and heading this way — especially in July and August. Not wanting to be on an exposed ridge during a lightning storm, it is wise to hurry down the trail to timberline and pitch a tent in the area around Cached Lake. Of all places encountered on this trip, this area is one to return to for cave exploring and general rock hounding. Even on a quick hike through the area one can see many curious geological happenings. Total distance day six: 12.1 miles.

You reach Eagle Lake (G) on day seven early in the morning by descending into the Main Eagle drainage and connecting with Trail No. 1922. Continue circling east around Eagle Lake by crossing a small, handmade irrigation dam and bushwack up to the lowest saddle on the northeast end of the lake. It is fairly steep, but not impossible. Once you are on top of the saddle, you can easily spot Hidden and Moon lakes below. Care should be taken on the descent from the saddle not to slop or dislodge rocks that could be injurious to hikers below. At

Moon Lake, you'll be on Trail No. 1915 which continues 1.8 miles down into the East Eagle drainage where it intersects with Trail No. 1910. Follow this trail upstream until you connect with Trail No. 1947 to Frazier Pass. Look for small campsites next to East Eagle Creek. Total distance day seven: 6.2 miles with some bushwacking.

It is a straight shot to Horton Pass (H) for day eight on Trail No. 1910. Once at the pass, the trail changes to No. 1805 and there is a spur off to your right that connects with the Eagle Cap Summit Trail. You may choose to move on into the Lakes Basin a little further before stashing your pack and heading up to the summit of Eagle Cap at 9,595'. The view at the top is worth the trudge up but expect a lot of other folks doing the same. This is truly the central point of the wilderness area. The drainages of the Wallowa River, Hurricane Creek, the Lostine River, the Minam River, East Eagle Creek, and the Imnaha River all spiral away from this central peak. The Lakes Basin is perhaps the most popular spot in the wilderness area so don't be surprised by the crowds. You can choose an out of the way campsite on a bluff overlooking Mirror Lake. Total distance day eight: 6.5 miles.

If day nine is to be the last day of the trip, one can stay on Trail No. 1805 until it intersects with Trail No. 1661. Traveling to the right a few hundred feet brings one to Trail No. 1662 which heads down the beautiful glacial valley of the East Fork of the Lostine River (I). Hiking the gradual slope down the Lostine River for about 6.0 miles brings you to the trailhead at the end of the Lostine River Road. The Bowman Trail trailhead, where the trip started, is about 3.5 miles down the road. Total distance day nine: 10.5 miles — including 3.5 miles on the road.

COMMENTS: As one can figure, there are unlimited routes to choose for loop travel in the Eagle Cap Wilderness. Depending on your transportation, routes can take you from east to west or north to south. On this particular loop, if you have someone ferry your car, you can end the hike at Moss Springs or North Catherine Creek in Union County, Boulder Park on Main Eagle Creek or Cornucopia in Baker County, or at Indian Crossing on the Imnaha River or Wallowa Lake in Wallowa County. There are many options.

A few hints about extended travel in a wilderness area that you learn from this trip. Bring lots of mole skin for your feet. You may use every bit of it. You can make the mistake of not bringing enough bug dope. Don't sell yourself short on food or drink. Bring some "Gatorade" type of powdered drink. It is amazing how after several days on the trail, a small drink of sugar water can really pick you up. Bring lots of film even if you aren't a camera fanatic. You'll be working hard to make those summits and mountain passes and should have something to show for it! Besides — pictures provide needed relief from cabin fever in the dead of winter.

Flagstaff Point. Twin Peaks in background. (Bob Jackson photo)

BIBLIOGRAPHY

Bartlett, Grace. *From the Wallowas*. Enterprise, Oregon.
    Pika Press, 1992

Carrey, Conley, Barton. *Snake River of Hells Canyon*.
    Cambridge, Idaho. Backeddy Books, 1979.

Douglas, William O. *Of Men and Mountains*. Seattle,
    Washington. Chronicle Books, 1992.

McArthur, Lewis A. *Oregon Geographic Names*. 6th Edition.
    Portland, Oregon. Oregon Historical Society, 1992.

Stevenson, Elmo. *Nature Rambles in the Wallowas,* reprint of
    1937 edition published by Metropolitan Press of
    Portland. Enterprise, Oregon. Pika Press, 1985.